W9-ATB-371

WITHDRAWN

FRANKLIN PARK PUBLIC LIBRARY
FRANKLIN PARK, ILL.

Each borrower is held responsible for all library material drawn on his card and for fines accruing on the same. No material will be issued until such fine has been paid.

All injuries to library material beyond reasonable wear and all losses shall be made good to the satisfaction of the Librarian.

MAJOR WORLD LEADERS

Fidel
Castro

Vicki Cox

CHELSEA HOUSE
PUBLISHERS
A Haights Cross Communications Company

Philadelphia

CHELSEA HOUSE PUBLISHERS

V.P., NEW PRODUCT DEVELOPMENT Sally Cheney
DIRECTOR OF PRODUCTION Kim Shinners
CREATIVE MANAGER Takeshi Takahashi
MANUFACTURING MANAGER Diann Grasse

Staff for FIDEL CASTRO

EXECUTIVE EDITOR Lee Marcott
SENIOR EDITOR Tara Koellhoffer
PRODUCTION ASSISTANT Megan Emery
PICTURE RESEARCH 21st Century Publishing and Communications, Inc.
SERIES DESIGNER Takeshi Takahashi
COVER DESIGNER Keith Trego
LAYOUT 21st Century Publishing and Communications, Inc.

A Haights Cross Communications ✦ Company

http://www.chelseahouse.com

First Printing

1 3 5 7 9 8 6 4 2

Library of Congress Cataloging-in-Publication Data

Cox, Vicki.
    Fidel Castro/by Vicki Cox ; foreword on leadership, Arthur Schlesinger, jr.
        p. cm.—(Major world leaders)
Summary: A biography of the man who has ruled Cuba since 1959, after leading a successful revolution overthrowing Batista's government and establishing a Communist regime in its place. Includes bibliographical references and index.
    ISBN 0-7910-7651-2
    1. Castro, Fidel, 1926- —Juvenile literature. 2. Cuba—History—1933-1959—Juvenile literature. 3. Cuba—History—1959—-Juvenile literature. 4. Heads of state—Cuba—Biography—Juvenile literature. 5. Revolutionaries—Cuba—Biography—Juvenile literature. [1. Castro, Fidel, 1927- 2. Heads of state. 3. Revolutionaries. 4. Cuba—History.] I. Title. II. Series.
F1788.22.C3C69 2003
972.9106'4'092—dc21

                                                                    2003013671

TABLE OF CONTENTS

On Leadership

Arthur M. Schlesinger, jr.

Leadership, it may be said, is really what makes the world go round. Love no doubt smoothes the passage; but love is a private transaction between consenting adults. Leadership is a public transaction with history. The idea of leadership affirms the capacity of individuals to move, inspire, and mobilize masses of people so that they act together in pursuit of an end. Sometimes leadership serves good purposes, sometimes bad; but whether the end is benign or evil, great leaders are those men and women who leave their personal stamp on history.

Now, the very concept of leadership implies the proposition that individuals can make a difference. This proposition has never been universally accepted. From classical times to the present day, eminent thinkers have regarded individuals as no more than the agents and pawns of larger forces, whether the gods and goddesses of the ancient world or, in the modern era, race, class, nation, the dialectic, the will of the people, the spirit of the times, history itself. Against such forces, the individual dwindles into insignificance.

So contends the thesis of historical determinism. Tolstoy's great novel *War and Peace* offers a famous statement of the case. Why, Tolstoy asked, did millions of men in the Napoleonic Wars, denying their human feelings and their common sense, move back and forth across Europe slaughtering their fellows? "The war," Tolstoy answered, "was bound to happen simply because it was bound to happen." All prior history determined it. As for leaders, they, Tolstoy said, "are but the labels that serve to give a name to an end and, like labels, they have the least possible connection with the event." The greater the leader, "the more conspicuous the inevitability and the predestination of every act he commits." The leader, said Tolstoy, is "the slave of history."

Determinism takes many forms. Marxism is the determinism of class. Nazism the determinism of race. But the idea of men and women as the slaves of history runs athwart the deepest human instincts. Rigid determinism abolishes the idea of human freedom—the assumption of free choice that underlies every move we make, every word we speak, every thought we think. It abolishes the idea of human responsibility, since it is manifestly unfair to reward or punish people for actions that are by definition beyond their control. No one can live consistently by any deterministic creed. The Marxist states prove this themselves by their extreme susceptibility to the cult of leadership.

More than that, history refutes the idea that individuals make no difference. In December 1931 a British politician crossing Fifth Avenue in New York City between 76th and 77th Streets around 10:30 P.M. looked in the wrong direction and was knocked down by an automobile— a moment, he later recalled, of a man aghast, a world aglare: "I do not understand why I was not broken like an eggshell or squashed like a gooseberry." Fourteen months later an American politician, sitting in an open car in Miami, Florida, was fired on by an assassin; the man beside him was hit. Those who believe that individuals make no difference to history might well ponder whether the next two decades would have been the same had Mario Constasino's car killed Winston Churchill in 1931 and Giuseppe Zangara's bullet killed Franklin Roosevelt in 1933. Suppose, in addition, that Lenin had died of typhus in Siberia in 1895 and that Hitler had been killed on the Western Front in 1916. What would the 20th century have looked like now?

For better or for worse, individuals do make a difference. "The notion that a people can run itself and its affairs anonymously," wrote the philosopher William James, "is now well known to be the silliest of absurdities. Mankind does nothing save through initiatives on the part of inventors, great or small, and imitation by the rest of us—these are the sole factors in human progress. Individuals of genius show the way, and set the patterns, which common people then adopt and follow."

Leadership, James suggests, means leadership in thought as well as in action. In the long run, leaders in thought may well make the greater difference to the world. "The ideas of economists and political philosophers, both when they are right and when they are wrong," wrote John Maynard Keynes, "are more powerful than is commonly understood. Indeed the world is ruled by little else. Practical men, who believe themselves to be quite exempt from any intellectual influences, are usually the slaves of some defunct economist. . . . The power of vested interests is vastly exaggerated compared with the gradual encroachment of ideas."

But, as Woodrow Wilson once said, "Those only are leaders of men, in the general eye, who lead in action. . . . It is at their hands that new thought gets its translation into the crude language of deeds." Leaders in thought often invent in solitude and obscurity, leaving to later generations the tasks of imitation. Leaders in action—the leaders portrayed in this series—have to be effective in their own time.

And they cannot be effective by themselves. They must act in response to the rhythms of their age. Their genius must be adapted, in a phrase from William James, "to the receptivities of the moment." Leaders are useless without followers. "There goes the mob," said the French politician, hearing a clamor in the streets. "I am their leader. I must follow them." Great leaders turn the inchoate emotions of the mob to purposes of their own. They seize on the opportunities of their time, the hopes, fears, frustrations, crises, potentialities. They succeed when events have prepared the way for them, when the community is awaiting to be aroused, when they can provide the clarifying and organizing ideas. Leadership completes the circuit between the individual and the mass and thereby alters history.

It may alter history for better or for worse. Leaders have been responsible for the most extravagant follies and most monstrous crimes that have beset suffering humanity. They have also been vital in such gains as humanity has made in individual freedom, religious and racial tolerance, social justice, and respect for human rights.

There is no sure way to tell in advance who is going to lead for good and who for evil. But a glance at the gallery of men and women in MAJOR WORLD LEADERS suggests some useful tests.

One test is this: Do leaders lead by force or by persuasion? By command or by consent? Through most of history leadership was exercised by the divine right of authority. The duty of followers was to defer and to obey. "Theirs not to reason why/Theirs but to do and die." On occasion, as with the so-called enlightened despots of the 18ᵗʰ century in Europe, absolutist leadership was animated by humane purposes. More often, absolutism nourished the passion for domination, land, gold, and conquest and resulted in tyranny.

The great revolution of modern times has been the revolution of equality. "Perhaps no form of government," wrote the British historian James Bryce in his study of the United States, *The American Commonwealth*, "needs great leaders so much as democracy." The idea that all people should be equal in their legal condition has undermined the old structure of authority, hierarchy, and deference. The revolution of equality has had two contrary effects on the nature of leadership. For equality, as Alexis de Tocqueville pointed out in his great study *Democracy in America*, might mean equality in servitude as well as equality in freedom.

"I know of only two methods of establishing equality in the political world," Tocqueville wrote. "Rights must be given to every citizen, or none at all to anyone . . . save one, who is the master of all." There was no middle ground "between the sovereignty of all and the absolute power of one man." In his astonishing prediction of 20th-century totalitarian dictatorship, Tocqueville explained how the revolution of equality could lead to the *Führerprinzip* and more terrible absolutism than the world had ever known.

But when rights are given to every citizen and the sovereignty of all is established, the problem of leadership takes a new form, becomes more exacting than ever before. It is easy to issue commands and enforce them by the rope and the stake, the concentration camp and the *gulag*. It is much harder to use argument and achievement to overcome opposition and win consent. The Founding Fathers of the United States understood the difficulty. They believed that history had given them the opportunity to decide, as Alexander Hamilton wrote in the first Federalist Paper, whether men are indeed capable of basing government on "reflection and choice, or whether they are forever destined to depend . . . on accident and force."

Government by reflection and choice called for a new style of leadership and a new quality of followership. It required leaders to be responsive to popular concerns, and it required followers to be active and informed participants in the process. Democracy does not eliminate emotion from politics; sometimes it fosters demagoguery; but it is confident that, as the greatest of democratic leaders put it, you cannot fool all of the people all of the time. It measures leadership by results and retires those who overreach or falter or fail.

It is true that in the long run despots are measured by results too. But they can postpone the day of judgment, sometimes indefinitely, and in the meantime they can do infinite harm. It is also true that democracy is no guarantee of virtue and intelligence in government, for the voice of the people is not necessarily the voice of God. But democracy, by assuring the right of opposition, offers built-in resistance to the evils inherent in absolutism. As the theologian Reinhold Niebuhr summed it up, "Man's capacity for justice makes democracy possible, but man's inclination to justice makes democracy necessary."

A second test for leadership is the end for which power is sought. When leaders have as their goal the supremacy of a master race or the promotion of totalitarian revolution or the acquisition and exploitation of colonies or the protection of greed and privilege or the preservation of personal power, it is likely that their leadership will do little to advance the cause of humanity. When their goal is the abolition of slavery, the liberation of women, the enlargement of opportunity for the poor and powerless, the extension of equal rights to racial minorities, the defense of the freedoms of expression and opposition, it is likely that their leadership will increase the sum of human liberty and welfare.

Leaders have done great harm to the world. They have also conferred great benefits. You will find both sorts in this series. Even "good" leaders must be regarded with a certain wariness. Leaders are not demigods; they put on their trousers one leg after another just like ordinary mortals. No leader is infallible, and every leader needs to be reminded of this at regular intervals. Irreverence irritates leaders but is their salvation. Unquestioning submission corrupts leaders and demeans followers. Making a cult of a leader is always a mistake. Fortunately hero worship generates its own antidote. "Every hero," said Emerson, "becomes a bore at last."

The signal benefit the great leaders confer is to embolden the rest of us to live according to our own best selves, to be active, insistent, and resolute in affirming our own sense of things. For great leaders attest to the reality of human freedom against the supposed inevitabilities of history. And they attest to the wisdom and power that may lie within the most unlikely of us, which is why Abraham Lincoln remains the supreme example of great leadership. A great leader, said Emerson, exhibits new possibilities to all humanity. "We feed on genius. . . . Great men exist that there may be greater men."

Great leaders, in short, justify themselves by emancipating and empowering their followers. So humanity struggles to master its destiny, remembering with Alexis de Tocqueville: "It is true that around every man a fatal circle is traced beyond which he cannot pass; but within the wide verge of that circle he is powerful and free; as it is with man, so with communities." ■

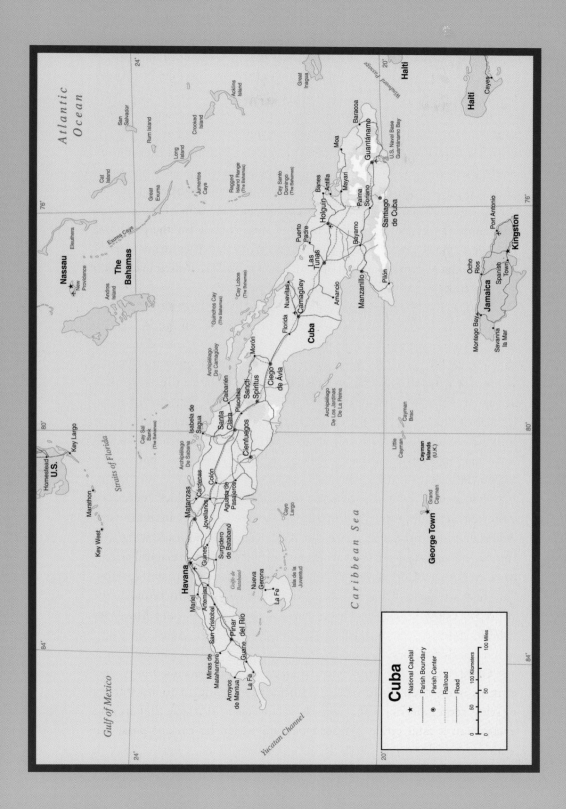

1

We Have Won!

Fidel Castro's army, all of 82 men, scattered in every direction. Some of his men were dead or bleeding in a Cuban sugarcane field. Some were cowering in the woods. Fragmentation bombs exploded around them. Armed soldiers roamed the area, searching for Castro and his men. Government aircraft flew above them. Hidden in a sugarcane field, covered with straw, Castro whispered to the two men beside him, "We are winning. . . . Victory will be ours."

Only Castro could look into complete defeat and still think he had triumphed. Though his guerrilla uniform was caked with mud, his face cut, and his beard dirty, Castro believed he was fulfilling his destiny and Cuba's. Being ambushed made no difference at all. He would overthrow dictator Fulgencio Batista's government. He would go right through its Rural Guard, national police, Sherman tanks, artillery, U.S.-supplied aircraft, and army of 40,000 soldiers. Castro

Fidel Castro (under the arrow) and 20 other Cuban exiles pose in front of a government office in Mexico City in June 1956. Five months later, Castro and a small rebel force set sail from Mexico for Cuba—in a trouble-plagued invasion.

believed he could conquer his opposition with a vision and hope that his fellow countrymen would join him in ending the cruelty and brutality of their president-turned-dictator.

Sixteen years before, in 1940, Batista had been elected the president of Cuba. Almost from the start, his government was corrupt. His police officers took kickbacks and were involved with prostitution, gambling, and drug rings. All commercial establishments paid contributions to the local precincts. When his four-year term ended, Batista left Cuba for Florida, watching while two other presidents, Ramon Grau San Martin and Carlos Prio Socarras, shredded the country even more. Batista wanted to run Cuba once again. Knowing he would not win office in free elections, he orchestrated a military coup that overthrew Prio, the outgoing president.

Once he seized the presidency in 1952, Batista censored newspapers, television, and radio. He banned elections and placed restrictions on opposition parties. Torture and imprisonment without a trial were common. The political parties had no strong leader to stand up to him and no plan to oppose him. The only real opposition to the Batista regime came in the university students' noisy, but short, demonstrations. Having exhausted all legal means to rid Cuba of its U.S.-backed dictator, Castro and a handful of Cubans realized that the only possible way to free Cuba from Batista was by armed revolution.

Castro had been moving toward his insurrection for four years, ever since Batista returned. He gave speeches, wrote articles, and led student demonstrations. He organized secret cells of soldiers. In Mexico, loyal young supporters trained to invade Cuba and overthrow Batista.

To look at the catastrophe in the cane fields and still think he had triumphed, Castro had to be a man with an enormous ego and unshakeable self-confidence—or else he was completely crazy. In fact, Castro had been called "*el loco*" before.

From its beginning in the fog-shrouded harbor of Tuxpan, Mexico, to the landing on Cuban soil, nothing had gone right in Castro's revolution. Because an informant had told the Mexican police about part of Castro's plan, some of his soldiers were arrested and their weapons were seized. Castro then hurriedly ordered his men to set sail on November 24, 1956. They left so unexpectedly that some of his followers did not know the expedition was really beginning. Once they saw the foul weather ahead of them, some didn't want to leave at all.

Castro's boat, the *Granma*, was hardly a vehicle worthy of a revolution. The rebels thought the dilapidated yacht, with its 25-person capacity, was a ferry to their real invasion boat. Its engine needed repair, its clutch slipped, and the bilge pump didn't work. Its one lifeboat was riddled with holes. Castro crowded 82 men, along with weapons and ammunition, on board. The boat was so overcrowded that only half the men could sit down; the other half stood. Water nearly lapped over the side.

Castro's forces were sailing to a destination 1,235 miles (1,988 kilometers) away. Entering the Gulf of Mexico, the men sang the Cuban national anthem and shouted, "*Viva la Revolución*" and "Down with the Batista dictatorship."

Then the northern winds whipped the little boat about violently. For two days, the liberators of the Cuban people forgot about glory and revolution. One participant later wrote that the men were "grabbing their stomachs; some with their heads inside buckets, others fallen in the strangest positions, motionless, their clothes filthy from vomit." Castro and three veteran seamen were the only ones not overcome by the heavy seas. The pump, which should have rid the boat of the crashing water, broke down. The men bailed furiously with buckets to keep afloat.

On November 26, they crept past the Yucatán Peninsula, and the weather improved. For all his vision of liberty and justice, Castro had not calculated on weather delays or on how much an overloaded boat would slow them down. Chugging along at eight miles (13 kilometers) per hour, the planned five-day-and-night trip stretched into seven. The men ran out of food, and before they landed, they would go two days without food or water.

More critical for Castro's revolution, the *Granma* was behind schedule by two days and 180 miles (290 kilometers). The revolutionaries should have arrived on November 30, at the same time that Frank Pais, a leader of the urban arm of Castro's so-called 26th of July Movement, attacked the city of Santiago. With 28 men, Pais attacked the customshouse, the police headquarters, and the harbor building to draw military units into the city and away from Castro's landing site. All the assault accomplished, however, were the deaths or capture of the rebels and an alert to the government about Castro's arrival.

On the *Granma*, mishaps continued as the boat neared

A billboard at the Plaza Martí in Havana shows the yacht *Granma*, on which Fidel Castro and 81 rebels returned to Cuba in late 1956. The dilapidated yacht was so overcrowded that only half the men could sit down.

Cuba. Searching for land, the boat's navigator, one of only three professional sailors manning the boat, fell overboard. Several hours were spent searching the seas for him. The delay cost Castro the last bit of cover that darkness would have provided the landing.

When Castro reached Cuba on December 2, the mission did not get any easier. The landing was literally a shipwreck. The *Granma* ran aground 100 yards (91 meters) off shore. Instead of departing like soldiers after pulling up to a pier, the men jumped into the water, carrying only personal items and small weapons. The heavy weapons, supplies, and the radio transmitter were stranded on the boat. The rebels also ended up a mile off target. Fifty local rebels were waiting at the appointed beach with jeeps and trucks to transport the equipment and Castro's men into the Sierra Maestra mountains. When Castro didn't appear, they left.

Coming ashore, the rebels discovered that they were in a mangrove swamp, wading in water up to their necks at times. Submerged trees tripped them, razor-sharp leaves lashed their faces, and mosquitoes attacked their skin. Castro led the way, holding his rifle above his head. The rebels struggled for two hours to walk a mile to firm ground. Some were so exhausted, they had to be carried.

Almost immediately, Batista's airplanes found the *Granma* and fired a bombardment of artillery into the mangrove swamp. A thousand men scoured the area, looking for Castro and his rag-tag group. The men struggled for three days through low brush and jagged volcanic rock to elude the government forces. Their shoes, ill-fitting and damaged from the swamp, produced blisters on their feet.

"We had landed too late and in the wrong place," one survivor said later. "Everything went wrong. That night we camped in a dense thicket with no food or water."

The second day, Castro and his men discovered a sugarcane field. They sucked on the cane for nourishment but thoughtlessly discarded the chewed stalks, leaving a trail behind them like Hansel and Gretel's bread crumbs. They marched east, guided by the son of a peasant who had given them rice and black beans in his hut. The guerrillas were so inexperienced, they never thought that the boy might betray their location to Batista's Rural Guard—which he did. Still marching east, Castro's band came upon a charcoal burners' village. A store owner gave them canned sausage and crackers. The path ahead of them turned into cane fields, where they could be spotted from the air. Castro decided to march at night.

On the morning of December 5, they reached Alegria de Pio near the Sierra Maestra mountains. The men were completely spent. They had stumbled, fallen, and fainted 22 miles (35 kilometers) from their landing site. Instead of ordering the men to move a few hundred more yards into a more protected area, Castro made camp on a low hill in a small grove of trees. He positioned sentries who, it turned out, set up too close to camp to provide any advance warning of an attack.

A little after 4:00 A.M., the men were awakened and given half a piece of sausage and two dry crackers. Several men had taken off their boots to wrap their bleeding feet. At 4:30, Batista's forces ambushed them, firing machine guns and rifles from two directions. Surrounded by nearly 400 men, Castro's men panicked, grabbing their boots, socks, and weapons. It was too late for thinking and obeying orders. Every man scrambled to save his own life. Some ran into the cane rows. Castro's good friend, Che Guevara, was wounded in the neck as he and four others escaped into the woods. They dodged napalm bombs dropped by aircraft.

Lost in the most rugged terrain in Cuba, they had no food or water for nine days. They survived by drinking their own urine and eating raw corn, crabs, and herbs. The rest scattered in 25 directions. The Rural Guard set the sugarcane field afire from two sides. The cane crackled. Cartridges exploded, heated by the flames. Bullets whizzed through the air, snapping twigs and leaves. Three men died in the sugarcane. Those who were captured were executed on the spot or killed later.

Castro and his two companions hid in a cane field for five days, finally leaving on December 10. They traveled only at night, marching through the rain and slithering through the muck and mire of a drainage ditch to reach their prearranged rendezvous point in the Sierra Maestra mountains. Along the way, peasants fed them and let them rest in their huts. Young men in the Sierra Maestra volunteered to join them.

Strangely, the more conditions deteriorated, the more

assured Castro became. "He was so confident we did not dare tell him we were not," one follower admitted. Although others suffered from the marches and lack of sleep, Castro's stamina seemed inexhaustible. Thirteen days after the cane field battle, Castro was reunited with his "army" of 13 men. When his brother, Raúl, entered their camp, Castro was overjoyed. Raúl had brought five rifles with him.

"With the two I have, this makes seven!" Castro exclaimed. "Now, yes, we have won the war!"

Only a man with larger-than-life dreams and energy to match could have survived such a disaster. All he had left was an army half the size of a football team and a few illiterate peasant sympathizers. Yet Fidel Castro was just the man the Cubans needed to restore their national pride and depose the brutal Batista. As Castro's men, the so-called Fidelistas, slipped into the misty blanket of the Sierra Maestra mountains, they were among the very few who believed that a new Cuba was possible. Only Fidel Castro was not surprised that its rebirth took just 25 months.

2

The Curses of Cuba: Spain, Sugar, and the United States

The stifling of Cuba's pride and national self-esteem began shortly after Christopher Columbus stepped ashore on October 27, 1492, and ended more than 450 years later with Castro's revolution. Cuba's conquerors, both external foreign powers and internal government officials, were always interested in how the island could benefit their country or their personal fortunes.

Early Spanish monarchs wanted something quite ordinary and finite from the island—gold. They saw the Taino Indians who inhabited the 745-mile-long (1,199-kilometer-long) island as a convenient labor force to harvest their treasure. Though they were a languid, hospitable people, the Taino resisted their conquerors. Some villagers committed mass suicide rather than submit to the Spanish. Others fought back, though their simple weapons were no match for the Spanish guns and horses. Once enslaved, the Taino

The Cuban coastline. By the early 1500s, the Spanish settlers realized that Cuba's wealth was in its lush vegetation, which included mahogany, cedar, and pomegranate forests. Fruits such as grapefruit, orange, lemon, mango, guava, and papaya were found across the land.

simply had no defense against the hard labor of "washing for gold" or the diseases that the Europeans brought with them. Within a century, the native population dwindled from 100,000 to a mere 4,000. To bolster its disappearing labor force, the Spanish imported slaves from Africa.

In the early 1500s, the Spanish finally realized that Cuba's real wealth was in the soil that produced its lush vegetation. For good reason, Columbus had called Cuba "the most beautiful land that human eyes have ever seen." Graceful palm trees, and mahogany, cedar, and pomegranate forests grew in the tropical temperatures. Grapefruits, oranges, lemons, cashews, coconuts, avocados, mangoes, guavas, and papayas spread across Cuba's nearly 43,000 square miles (69,202 square kilometers). Three hundred species of birds fluttered through the trees, while 4,000 species of mollusks and 500 species of fish waited in the temperate waters.

Cuba was turned into a huge Spanish garden. At first, raising cattle, fed on Cuba's grasses, was a prime industry. Salted meat was sold to Spanish ships in Cuba's ports. Leather goods made from cow hides for the European market also proved profitable.

Cuban soil was especially good for growing tobacco, which was a popular commodity in the seventeenth and eighteenth centuries. Europeans demanded it, and the tobacco farms required only a small labor force. Spain set up a strict monopoly, requiring independent farmers to sell at a very low price and reselling the tobacco to Europe at a high profit.

Cuba's strategic location also made it a stepping stone to the riches of the New World. Spain sent Cortés into Mexico and de Soto into Florida from Cuba's shores. For explorers returning to Spain with their treasures, Cuba provided a safe harbor to assemble at before the long and dangerous trip home. To protect its ships from English, French, and Dutch pirates, Spain fortified Havana Harbor and developed a flota system so its ships traveled between the Americas and Spain in a group. Buccaneers, who worked for whichever country would pay them the biggest purse, harassed anything Spanish. Henry Morgan, one of the most infamous buccaneers, butchered and tortured Cuban Spaniards in the Oriente and Camaguey provinces.

The Spanish introduced sugarcane from India and New

Guinea. The sugar industry grew slowly because Spain could not absorb all of Cuba's sugar itself and would not allow other nations to trade with its prize colony. However, three unrelated events changed sugar's status quo. First, Great Britain attacked and took possession of Cuba in 1762 (although Spain later took back the island). Second, the United States won its independence from Britain, creating an important market for Cuban products. Third, a slave rebellion in Haiti destroyed most of that island's sugar and coffee estates, opening a market up for Cuban sugar. Sugar production nearly doubled between 1790 and 1805, when Cuba produced 24,000 tons of sugar. Sugar mills increased to 478 (twice the number from before the English takeover). The large cattle estates were divided into smaller sugar and coffee farms. When the coffee industry collapsed, coffee land turned into cane fields. By 1860, 2,000 sugar mills dotted the island.

The demand for sugar cut into the forests as farms expanded into plantations and then into large estates. The tall stalks of sugarcane eliminated other food crops that Cuba needed to be self-sufficient. Cuba was forced to buy supplies, primarily from mother Spain.

Just 90 miles (145 kilometers) away, newly independent Americans were aware of Cuba and thought it ought to be theirs instead of belonging to a country far across the Atlantic Ocean. John Quincy Adams described Cuba as "an apple that had to fall by gravity into the hands of the United States." Presidents James K. Polk, Franklin Pierce, and James Buchanan tried repeatedly to buy Cuba from Spain, but the great Spanish Empire refused. In 1854, a secret report called the "Ostend Manifesto" proposed that the United States either buy the island or take it forcibly. Some Cuban businessmen and supporters of slavery preferred annexation by the United States to the dominance of Spain.

Although its empire crumbled elsewhere, Spain was determined to hang on to its Cuban colony. It successfully

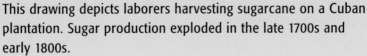

This drawing depicts laborers harvesting sugarcane on a Cuban plantation. Sugar production exploded in the late 1700s and early 1800s.

quelled the few rebellions that various Cuban groups started—until 1868.

Midway through the nineteenth century, Cubans were weary of Spanish control. Though some representatives of the throne governed Cuba fairly, others were cruel and oppressive. Knowing that so many other Spanish possessions had become independent, Cuban factions finally united to mount a full-scale insurrection.

With the cry, "*Grito de Yaro*," the wealthy Oriente land-owner Carlos Cespedes led lawyers, professionals, peasants, and slaves against Spain. The rebels wanted complete independence, equal rights for all, and freedom for the slaves. The Cubans won early battles. Their most effective tactic was "*la guerrilla*," or the "little warfare," maneuvers. Fidel Castro would adopt the strategy 90 years later to bring down Fulgencio Batista's government.

The Ten Years' War of Independence dragged on, resulting in 200,000 dead on both sides and the destruction of the island. In the end, Spain, with its well-trained soldiers and navy, maintained control over Cuba.

The Cuban cause was harmed most by quarreling among the rebels, jealousies among the leadership, and a general lack of organization. Castro, a student of history, would not make these mistakes when he mounted his own campaign.

If anything, the years of fighting from 1868 to 1879 harmed the dream of a self-ruled Cuba more than helped it. American entrepreneurs bought up many of Cuba's sugar estates and mining interests at bargain prices from Cuban and Spanish businesses. With diminishing European markets, the United States became Cuba's primary buyer of sugar. When the fighting ceased, Spain still controlled Cuba's politics, but the influence of the United States on Cuba's economy increased.

In 1895, Cuba found its first Cuban hero in Jose Martí and his cry of "*Cuba Libre!*" As a teenager, the country's "Apostle of Freedom" began writing poetry and essays about a free Cuba. He was arrested, sentenced to hard labor at the age of 16, and finally deported to Spain. An intellectual and an idealist, he completed a philosophy and law degree and worked as a journalist, finally settling in New York. His real passion was an independent Cuba, to be achieved through revolution. His dream was a republican government, where wealth and land would be distributed equally. He also wanted to break the sugar industry's hold on Cuba. He feared that the United States would intervene in a war of independence, tying Cuba more strongly to it. His writings would strongly influence Castro, who linked his plans and ideas to those of Cuba's first national hero and martyr.

Martí helped form the Cuban Revolutionary Party. With rebel forces, he entered Cuba on April 11, 1895, in the Oriente Province. Thirty-nine days later, Martí was dead. Conspicuous on a white horse, he rode into a small skirmish with the Spanish and was, predictably, shot. He never lived to see his anti-Spanish troops push the larger and better-armed enemy back through Cuban provinces toward Havana.

The Cubans seemed near victory when Spain sent General Valeriano Weyler to the island. To prevent the rural people from helping the rebels, he ordered the evacuation of the entire rural population to the cities. Hundreds of thousands of people starved to death on the streets as a result of "the Butcher's" actions. Still, he could not defeat the Cuban rebels, who retreated to the eastern provinces and carried on guerrilla operations against him.

Though the United States officially maintained a neutral position in the Spanish-Cuban conflict, it itched to enter the war. President William C. McKinley called Weyler's tactics "an extermination." The United States wanted to protect American interests in Cuba, it wanted Cuba as a market for its industrial goods, and it needed Cuba to protect the Isthmus of Panama. The mysterious explosion of the U.S.S. *Maine* in Havana Harbor on February 15, 1898, gave the United States an excuse to go to war against Spain. The beleaguered empire then faced two enemies: Cuban rebels and the United States.

Meanwhile, in Galicia, a desolate Spanish province, a young man named Angel Castro made a decision that would eventually change Cuba's destiny. In return for thousands of pesetas, Castro, a poor boy in a poor province, took the place

The first American troops land on a beach in Cuba at the start of the Spanish-American War in 1898. In essence, the war handed control of Cuba from one foreign country, Spain, to another, the United States.

of a rich Spanish boy who was scheduled to fight in faraway Cuba. Had Angel not gone to fight in Cuba and emigrated there after the war, his son, Fidel, might have grown up as just another poor Spaniard.

The Spanish-American War was not much of a conflict.

The only significant battle occurred on July 1, 1898, when future U.S. President Theodore Roosevelt and his "Rough Riders" fought their way up San Juan Hill. Roosevelt wrote: "Yesterday we struck the Spaniards and had a brisk fight for two and a half hours. The Spaniards shot well, but they did not stand when we rushed."

The Cubans, who had fought so bravely for their own independence, were never allowed to share the victory. The Americans rode into Santiago alone. When the Spanish flag was lowered in surrender, the Stars and Stripes was raised over the governor's palace. In essence, the Spanish-American War merely handed control of Cuba from one foreign country to another.

The American military took complete charge of the country, forcing the rebels to disband. Four years later, in 1902, the United States agreed to withdraw from Cuban soil, provided that Cuba accepted a constitution written by the United States. Besides denying voting rights to black Cubans, the document included an amendment that bound Cuba to the United States just as tightly as any Spanish manacle had.

The Platt Amendment, as the document that established the U.S. relationship with Cuba was called, had some provisions that Cubans considered very insulting. It said that the United States had the right to intervene militarily in Cuba's internal affairs, that Cuba must lease land to America for a naval base, and that Cuba must clean up its cities to reduce the risk of disease and epidemics to the United States. Some Cubans saw the new "Cuban" constitution for what it really was. Juan Gualberto Gomez wrote, "The Platt Amendment has reduced the independence and sovereignty of the Cuban republic to a myth."

With Cuban agreement to its demands, the United States relinquished control of the island. For the first time, Cuba was, at least in name, a bona fide country, with a

Cuban leader in President Tomás Estrada Palma. The new country celebrated its freedom. It should have recalled Martí's earlier question: Once the United States is in Cuba, who will get it out?

Little did anyone suspect that an anonymous soldier in the ranks of the conquered Spanish troops would sire the answer.

3

Growing up and Going to School

The second son of Angel Maria Castro and Lina Ruz Gonzalez was born bigger than life. Fidel Alejandro Castro Ruz weighed in at a whopping 12 pounds (five kilograms), inheriting his larger-than-life personality from his flamboyant parents.

In 1905, his father, a mercenary in the Spanish-American War, immigrated to Cuba from Galicia, a forlorn province in Spain. Tall and strong, the Gallego was a hard worker. He was employed in the nickel mines of Santiago and by the United Fruit Company, the huge American firm that owned 240,000 acres (97,125 hectares) of the Oriente Province. Starting out as a cane cutter, he eventually became foreman. He also prepared railroad beds by forming his own groups of workers and bought oxen to transport sugarcane. With his savings, he bought land. He also enlarged his property by "moving fences" between his land and unclaimed land. By the time

Fidel Castro with his mother, Lina, right, in September 1960 before Castro left for New York City to address a session of the United Nations.

Fidel was born on August 13, 1926, his father had acquired a sugar and cattle plantation that encompassed 23,000 acres (9,308 hectares).

Angel was married with two children when he hired a friend's 14-year-old daughter, Lina, as a maid. His affair with Lina prompted Angel's wife to leave "Las Manacas," the Castro plantation. Angel's mistress—Fidel's mother—bore seven children, two before Fidel and four after.

Lina Ruz liked high boots and loose, revealing dresses, and riding around the Castro plantation on horseback. Unlike other wealthy women, she managed the house herself, firing off a shotgun to announce dinner. The family's only cooked meal of the day fed everyone. Angel and the field hands ladled their food from a large pot on the stove. They used their hands and teeth to tear off chunks of meat from their plates.

Ramón, Fidel's older brother, described their mother as "afraid of nothing. She could kill a cow. She had veterinary knowledge and vaccinated the swine. She was the best rider."

The Castros' large house was built on stilts, Spanish-style. Pigs and poultry were kept under it, along with 20 to 30 cows. A small slaughterhouse, a smithy, a bakery, cockfighting pit, general store, and post office were nearby.

Fidel's schooling began early in a small schoolhouse about 60 meters (66 yards) down the dirt road from his home. Sitting at a desk in the front row, Fidel learned to read and write before his fifth birthday. "They sent me there when I was very young," Castro recalled in 1998. "They had nothing else to do with me, so they sent me there with my older sister and brother."

Even in kindergarten, Fidel was aware of the differences between him and his classmates. His father's wealth provided Fidel with shoes, while his classmates went barefoot. But, despite his economic status, the Catholic community was well aware that Fidel's family was a "broken" one and that Fidel was illegitimate.

Castro himself admits that he was every teacher's nightmare, challenging authority: "I remember that whenever I disagreed with something the teacher said to me or whenever I got mad, I would swear at her and immediately leave school, running as fast as I could. There was a kind of standing war between me and the teacher."

His teacher, a Señorita Felieu, convinced his parents that Fidel was very bright and would benefit from schooling in Santiago. They sent the six-year-old, along with Ramón and Angelita, to live with the teacher's sister. It was an unhappy time for young Fidel, who felt abandoned by his family. His schooling consisted of memorizing mathematics tables printed on the inside of his notebook.

Things improved when his parents enrolled him in La Salle, a Catholic school located a short distance from where he stayed. This decision required Fidel's parents to marry and their children to be baptized. Their marriage eliminated some of the bad names children had been calling him.

As a day student who returned each evening to his guardians, he missed the extra activities at the school. "I made up my mind then and proceeded to rebel and insult everybody," Fidel recalled. "I behaved so terribly that they took me straight back to school. It was a great victory. I wasn't alone anymore."

Some of his problems moved with him to the school. He did not like the absolute authority of the priests. His family was well off, but as the son of a peasant, he was not included in the circle of the upper-class wealthy. He was disruptive, pushing and shoving to be the first in line, demanding to be the pitcher in baseball games, and throwing desks when he was punished. Writing "I will not talk in line" and "I'll behave in line" thousands of times inspired no improvement.

Raúl, Fidel's younger brother, remembers him differently. "He succeeded in everything," Raúl said. "In sports, in studies. And every day he would fight. He had a very explosive character. He challenged the biggest and the strongest ones, and when he was beaten, he started it all over again the next day. He would never quit."

The priests told their father that Fidel and his two brothers, Ramón and Raúl, were the "three biggest bullies" ever to attend the school. Fed up, their father brought the boys home, intending to end their education. Fidel later called the incident "a decisive moment in my life." He threw tantrums and appealed to his mother to allow him to go back to school, threatening to burn the house down if she did not. Eventually, Lina persuaded Fidel's father to reconsider, and Fidel went to Dolores College, a Jesuit school.

Not prepared for the stiffer standards at the new school, and recovering from an infection caused by an appendectomy, he did not do well academically. The enterprising fifth-grader

Fidel, shown eating a lollipop, with classmates in 1940 at a Catholic school in Santiago, Cuba. When he was a fifth-grader, he kept two report cards, one from the teacher and one he made himself for his parents to sign.

hid his failures from his parents by keeping two sets of report cards, one from the teacher and one he made himself.

In the sixth grade, he became interested in history and geography. He learned about Cuba's great men—Antonio Maceo, Calixto Garcia, and Jose Martí. Boarding this time with a business friend of his father's, he was often locked in his room. His guardian expected Fidel to do well. Fidel said, "If I did not get the highest grade, I didn't get that week's 10 cents for going to the movies, five cents for buying ice cream after the movies, and five cents on Thursday for buying some comic books."

Homework was no punishment for Fidel. He just took the opportunity to invent battle games, created with little pieces of paper and a playing board. "I did stay there for hours, but without studying anything," he said. Instead he would "fly off to places and events in history and to wars."

Finally becoming a live-in student, Fidel found an acceptable way to channel his aggressive energy. "I always liked sports," Castro said. "For me, sports were a diversion, and I put my energy into them." He played soccer, basketball, baseball, and volleyball.

There was nothing shy about Fidel. In 1940, the 14-year-old wrote a letter to Franklin D. Roosevelt congratulating the U.S. president on his election to a third term and asking for an autographed $20 bill. He added that if Roosevelt wanted iron to build ships, Fidel would "show you the biggest [sic] mines of iron of the land." The president responded with thanks but sent no money or advisors to get the ore.

In 1942, Fidel moved on to Colegio de Belen in Havana, one of the best schools in the country. At 16, as a high school junior, he arrived in Cuba's capital for the first time. His mentor, Father Llorente, remembered him as a good student: "He was not deep. He was intuitive." Father Llorente also saw glimpses of his father's Spanish heritage. Fidel "had the cruelty of the Gallego. The Cuban is courtly. The Cuban would give up before he made people suffer. The Spaniard of the north is cruel, hard," Llorente said.

The Jesuit priests corralled Fidel's kinetic energy. He was placed in the Exploradores, an elite group of students who showed particular potential. Similar to the Boy Scouts, the

Exploradores camped out in the wilderness and climbed mountains during three-to-five-day excursions. Fidel was elected their leader and once saved a priest, who had fallen into a raging river.

His teachers introduced him to the world of books and the pursuit of knowledge. He applied his considerable powers of concentration to subjects that interested him. Those that did not, such as French or logic, he nearly failed. He learned the styles and behaviors of dictators, like Mussolini, Hitler, Primo de Rivera, Lenin, and Stalin, as well as of Cuba's hero, Jose Martí. Communism, when it was mentioned, was described in negative terms. Castro recalled, "I got good grades, even though my attention wandered in class and I had the bad habit of depending on last-minute cramming."

Standing six feet tall and weighing 190 pounds (86 kilograms), he was a formidable opponent on the basketball court. At first, he did not know how to play and was cut after his first tryout. Failure did not sit well with the young Castro, however. He practiced so much at night that the priests finally installed lights on the outdoor basketball court. Working his way onto the team, he wanted to win so badly, he sometimes forgot which team he was on and made baskets for both. An argument with a referee once caused a brawl among the players. The school coach later said, "Fidel drove me crazy, always asking me what he had to do to be a leader, what he had to do to make himself known."

Baseball scouts were also impressed by Fidel's athletic prowess. He was invited to the Washington Senators' tryout camps.

Despite being the school's team captain, Fidel lived a solitary existence. Off the court, students remembered he was wealthy, but still the son of a peasant. Fidel was not often invited to friends' homes, nor was he inclined to take teammates to his. That mattered little to him. He did not adjust his personality to fit his environment. Fidel, the child,

In 1945, Fidel Castro was chosen as the best athlete at Colegio de Belen. Besides basketball, he was also skilled at baseball and was invited to the Washington Senators' tryout camp.

rode his bike into a brick wall to prove he could do things no one else could do. His school years merely showed him ways to find the spotlight. He liked standing head and shoulders above the others. It did not matter if he stood there alone.

4

Finding a Cause

The governments that ruled Cuba while Fidel Castro was growing up were riddled with corruption and ruthlessness. Four presidents—Gerardo Machado, Carlos Cespedes, Fulgencio Batista, and Ramon Grau San Martin—invariably veered from reform intentions into graft. The people, frustrated by their leaders, formed gangs called "*grupos de acción*" to hand out their own justice.

For a while, Grau instituted new programs, trying to eliminate foreign influences in Cuba. He wanted more Cubans in labor organizations and signed a decree requiring all business enterprises to hire at least 50 percent native Cubans. His regime became increasingly corrupt, though. Students vented their frustration in violent demonstrations. Each time the army (now headed by Batista) quelled an uprising, it grew more powerful.

At the University of Havana, students formed their own gangs. Castro later said that his five years there were "much more dangerous than all the time I fought against Batista from the Sierra Maestra." The self-proclaimed "revolutionaries" were responsible for many murders and beatings. Little could be done because the campus was off-limits to the police and the army. President Grau even hired two campus gangs, the Insurrectional Revolutionary Union (URI) and the Socialist Revolutionary Movement (MSR), to terrorize or eliminate his enemies.

Castro arrived in this environment in October 1945, driving up in a new Ford V-8. He dressed in pin-striped suits and gaudy ties instead of the usual sports shirts. Blessed with good looks and powerfully built, he was hard to ignore. Instead of being impressed, though, young aristocrats disdainfully nicknamed him "Greaseball."

A campus teeming with political unrest excited him. Rather than settling down quietly to study law as his parents expected, Castro quickly became involved in university politics. He spent a lot of time talking at cafés, spinning his theories of government reform. One student recalled, "He talked politics all the time, *all* the time, with a very, very grandiose, and at the same time, idealistic scheme of how to run the country, how to improve things. He did it with a great deal of passion, emotion, vehemence—convincing people. . . ."

Castro was elected to be a freshman law school representative. Quickly, he focused on becoming student body president. Both the URI and the MSR courted him for his leadership abilities. For a while he wavered between them, hoping one or the other would help him win the student body presidency. He supposedly shot a URI member to ingratiate himself with the MSR. The MSR did not invite him to join, though, and the URI, impressed by his defense of his attempted murder of one of their members, invited him to join. One companion later wrote, "He was a combination genius and juvenile delinquent;

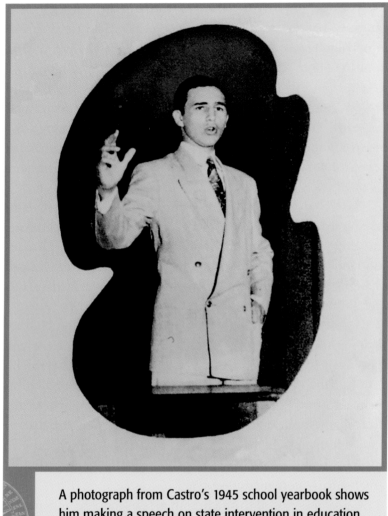

A photograph from Castro's 1945 school yearbook shows him making a speech on state intervention in education. His political activity increased when he began to attend the University of Havana in October 1945.

one moment, he would show signs of brilliance, and the next, he would behave like a hoodlum."

Castro tried to rise in the ranks of university politics. His charismatic personality gained him friends, but no student organization, including the Communists, would support him.

He was too volatile, unpredictable, and uncontrollable. He had worked hard to revise the rules so the Student Federation president could be elected by popular vote. When his proposal (and his chance at becoming student president) failed, he turned to national and international concerns.

On May 15, 1947, the 20-year-old Castro joined Eduardo Chibas. His new party, the Party of the Cuban People (Ortodoxos) emphasized nationalism, anti-imperialism, socialism, economic independence, political liberty, and social justice.

Castro also took bayonet practice for his first venture into international politics. Castro joined Cuban, Dominican, Venezuelan, and Costa Rican idealists in planning the overthrow of the Dominican Republic's brutal dictator, Rafael Trujillo. The so-called Cayo Confites expedition never reached the Dominican Republic. Its plans were so public that even the object of the overthrow, Trujillo, knew about them.

The invasion boats were en route when a naval vessel intercepted them. Intervening in Cuban affairs, the United States pressured the Cuban government to step in. President Grau ordered the 1,200 participants arrested. As the boat sailed back to Havana, Castro jumped overboard, preferring a nine-mile (14.5-kilometer) swim in shark-infested waters to an encounter with his gang enemies or a Cuban jail.

Three days later, on September 30, Castro was back at the university, agitating against the government. He joined a crowd carrying the coffin of a young boy who was killed in a conflict between the students and a government official's motorcade. At the Presidential Palace, he addressed thousands, holding President Grau personally responsible for the boy's death. A few days later, Castro participated in a nationwide student strike.

Two months after the failed Dominican overthrow, he organized the move of the Bell of La Demajagua from the Oriente Province to the Presidential Palace in Havana. He thought a massive march to the palace with the bell that had rung as Cuba's war of independence started, would force Grau from power. Castro organized a demonstration against police brutality—which turned into a riot. Another of his demonstrations stressed nonviolence, even as students in the protest carried pistols. His name was linked, incorrectly, to the death of an MSR gang leader in February 1948. An opportunity to leave the country saved Castro's life.

In April 1948, Castro and three other Cubans joined student delegates from Latin America in Bogotá, Colombia. Sponsored by the Argentine dictator Juan Perón, the delegates were to plan a hemisphere-wide, anti-imperialist, anti-American student congress for the following fall. Once they arrived in Bogotá, they invited the popular Colombian leader, Jorge Gaitan, to speak at the conference. A follow-up appointment with him was set for 2:00 P.M. on April 9. Forty minutes before the meeting, however, Gaitan was gunned down as he was walking down the street. Hysterical mobs beat his murderer to death before he could be removed from the scene.

The frenzy that immediately followed Gaitan's death, which came to be called the "*Bogotazo*," lasted three days. People burned cars, overturned buses, wrecked streetlights, threw rocks, and shattered storefronts. While his Cuban associates headed for safety, Castro walked toward the mass violence to watch and learn. Later he would recall, "I join the first ranks of this crowd. I see there is a revolution erupting, and I decide to be part of it as one more person. . . ." The crowd headed to a police station, where an officer, sympathetic to the rioters, gave Castro a gun and 16 rounds of ammunition. Castro was swept along with the crowd toward the Presidential Palace and the radio station. When the government soldiers started shooting, he escaped to the university and then headed to another police station that had been captured.

Appalled by the protest's disorganization and looting, Castro asked to be taken to the rebel leaders. Just as the teenage

Protesting students at the University of Havana in November 1947 demand the resignation of Ramon Grau San Martin, the Cuban president. Castro was an organizer of several protests against the government at the time.

Castro had boldly offered to help President Roosevelt find iron ore, the adult Castro brazenly offered his leadership and knowledge of Cuban wars. No one accepted his offer.

Castro learned much from the "Bogotazo." Later, he claimed it led him to decide that "there would be no anarchy, no looting, no disorders . . . that the people would not take justice into their own hands" when his revolution triumphed.

Within a week of his return to Cuba, Castro was accused of murdering a university policeman. Until a witness recanted his accusation, Castro feared that the campus gangs or the university police would kill him. With his name finally cleared, he participated in a demonstration protesting bus-fare increases instituted by the outgoing president, Grau. Students seized eight buses and drove them to the university. When Castro and others hinted that there would be more trouble if the university's sanctity were violated, the administration quietly canceled the higher fares.

Early in 1948, Castro met Mirta Diaz-Balart in the law school cafeteria, and fell in love at first sight. The green-eyed, blond-haired beauty captured the heart of a man whose only previous thoughts had been about himself and politics. She, too, was infatuated by the handsome man her brother introduced to her. Both Castro and Mirta had grown up in Oriente Province—Castro in the rustic, ramshackle village of Biran and Mirta near the manicured grounds owned by the United Fruit Company. Both were young, wealthy, and educated.

The couple married on October 12, 1948, two days after a new president, Carlos Prio Socarras, was inaugurated. The groom carried a concealed gun during the ceremony, in case his gang enemies showed up. The couple enjoyed a three-month honeymoon, courtesy of a $10,000 wedding gift from Mirta's father. Not yet vehemently anti–United States, Castro took his bride to Florida, where he enjoyed steak and smoked salmon, and then to New York, where he bought an enormous white Lincoln Continental. He also bought his first copy of the famous Marxist tract *Das Kapital*.

Returning home, Castro soon went back to politics and began cramming for his law degree. His obsessions left little room for providing for his bride. He was not interested in a paying job; he was content to take money from his father and Mirta's. Their financial situation was often so desperate that the

Fidel Castro with his son, Felix Fidel "Fidelito" Castro Diaz, in their apartment in the Hilton Hotel in Havana in February 1959. The boy was born almost a year after Castro had married Mirta Diaz-Balart. The Castros would divorce in the mid-1950s.

electricity was sometimes turned off and their furniture repossessed for lack of payment. Their first child, Felix Fidel Castro Diaz, or "Fidelito," was born on September 14, 1949, but Castro had little time for family life. He was seldom home, preferring his friends and colleagues to his wife and child.

In Cuba, corruption in the government and resentment against the United States were always present. President Prio's administration was no better than the one it had replaced. Prio sold government jobs for political loyalty and favors. From 1943 to 1949, the number of government employees increased from 60,000 to 131,000. To control gang activity, Prio formed "pacts" with the gangs, essentially buying their cooperation with appointments and promises of amnesty.

Though government excesses and abuses preoccupied the citizenry, anti-American sentiment always simmered just under the surface of society. It exploded throughout Cuba in March 1949. A group of U.S. marines, on leave from the Guantánamo Bay Naval Base, got drunk in downtown Havana. One climbed on the statue of Jose Martí, the hero of the "new Cuba," and urinated on it. Cubans everywhere were insulted and outraged. Sensing a situation from which he could profit, Castro quickly formed an all-night honor guard around the statue. He rallied students for a protest at the U.S. Embassy. The mob threw rocks at the embassy building and demanded that the marines be turned over to Cuban authorities. Refusing such a suggestion, the U.S. ambassador tried to defuse the situation by apologizing for the incident and laying a wreath at the statue of Martí.

Angered by the arrangements between Prio's administration and the gangs, students formed the Thirtieth of September Committee. In order to join, Castro stopped carrying his pistol and denounced all those involved in the secret pacts. In a speech before the university presidents and 500 students, he named politicians, gangsters, and student leaders who profited from Prio's peace pacts. A prominent Ortodoxos leader quickly recognized the danger in which Castro had placed himself. Driving Castro off campus, he hid him for two weeks until Castro could slip out of Cuba for a few months.

Returning from New York, Castro was determined to finish his degree in 1950. He spent the spring and summer reading at home, rather than attending classes. His photographic memory helped him learn two years' work in six months. Castro graduated with Doctor of Law, Doctor of Social Science, and Doctor of Diplomatic Law degrees in September 1950. He founded a law firm called Azpiazu, Castro & Resende in a section of Old Havana. Although his connections with his wealthy in-laws could have set him up in a productive practice, Castro took only cases involving some political issue or lost cause. His clients were common people of the working class.

5

Moncada: The Mother of the Revolution

Castro's law practice was secondary to his activities with the Ortodoxos Party. Its leader, Eddy Chibas, was an honorable and popular man, who was heading toward high office when he attacked government corruption using specific names and crimes. Challenged to substantiate his claims that the minister of education had embezzled funds for his Guatemalan business dealings, a humiliated Chibas spoke on his weekly radio program. After defending himself, he pulled a .38-caliber pistol and shot himself in the abdomen. A horrified Castro stood nearby.

When Chibas died ten days later, Castro orchestrated the funeral, insisting that it take place in the sanctity of the university campus. He organized a 24-hour honor guard. Dressed in a formal gray suit and tie, he stood by the coffin all night. He even proposed inciting an overthrow of the government by taking Chibas's body to the Presidential Palace and placing it in President Prio's chair.

Castro wanted to run for the House of Representatives as an Ortodoxos. The party, however, would not support the unpredictable Castro. Campaigning on his own, he wrote letters (actually printed from a stencil) to 100,000 voters. They believed Castro had written them personally. He talked to many voters, some with an annual salary of only $108. Such campaigning surprised people. "This had never happened in Cuba before, in as much as political leaders simply went to rallies to deliver their speeches," an Ortodoxos leader said.

Castro also exposed President Prio's many corruptions. Posing as a gardener, Castro photographed the extravagances of the presidential villa. He revealed that Prio paid gangs 10,000 pesos a month and employed 2,000 people in phantom government jobs. Castro disclosed Prio's land increases, from 160 to 1,944 acres (65 to 787 hectares). People were astonished by these revelations.

Castro had every reason to believe he would be elected in June. The elections never happened, however. On March 10, 1952, Fulgencio Batista and the military overthrew Prio's government. By eliminating elections he knew he could not win, Batista crushed Castro's hope of reforming the government through legal processes.

Castro turned to different solutions to Cuba's problems. Six days after Batista's coup, Castro interrupted an Ortodoxos meeting at Chibas's tomb. Hearing one leader lobby for a quiet "civil resistance" against Batista, Castro jumped on a tombstone, arguing that only force could unseat a military dictatorship.

Castro then found a group that believed, as he did, that insurrection was the only alternative. He met Abel Santamaria and young professionals working at Cuban divisions of Pontiac, Frigidaire, and General Motors. They met regularly

Fulgencio Batista, at center behind the microphones, takes the oath of office as president of Cuba in 1940. He left office in 1944, and in 1952, returned to power through a military coup.

at Santamaria's apartment to talk. Castro later said, "My idea then was not to organize a movement, but to try to unite all the different forces against Batista. I intended to participate in the struggle simply as one more soldier. . . . But when none of these leaders showed they had either the ability or the seriousness of purpose, or the way to overthrow Batista, it was then I finally worked out a strategy of my own." Gradually, Castro assumed leadership responsibilities.

Santamaria's sister, Haydee, experienced the transformation. "Three days after Castro started coming to our apartment it was no longer Abel that I followed," she said. "It was Fidel. And only someone of tremendous personality and tremendous character can do that."

During the summer of 1952, Castro and Santamaria began planning an attack on Santiago's Moncada army barracks, Cuba's second-largest garrison. They recruited 1,200 18- and 19-year-olds from the working class. Perhaps because of the very public and ill-fated Trujillo overthrow attempt, Castro insisted upon the utmost secrecy. The ten-man cells knew little about each other. The groups traveled individually to the university and trained on the science building's roof until they moved to a two-acre (one-hectare) farm close to their target. Some recruits did not know that Castro headed their movement.

Strangely, Castro and 500 of his men joined a very public celebration of Jose Martí's birth on January 27, 1953. Carrying torches and marching shoulder to shoulder, the men shouted, "Revolution! Revolution! Revolution!" Spectators thought they were Communists. Batista's men barely noticed them in the parade.

Castro had targeted the Moncada barracks for its weapons. With little money, his movement could not purchase guns. Castro told his supporters, "There is no need to buy them. There is no need to bring them. . . . The only thing that needs to be done is to capture them."

The attack was scheduled for July 26, 1953, during Santiago's three-day religious festival. Castro expected military discipline to be low during the popular carnival. His 100 chosen revolutionaries were stunned at the plan. Armed with three U.S. army rifles, six Winchester rifles, revolvers, hunting rifles, and one machine gun, they were supposed to overwhelm a garrison of a thousand soldiers. The men would be split into three groups: One would attack the main gates with Castro; another, led by Santamaria, would seize the hospital; the third, headed by Castro's brother Raúl, would supply cover fire from the roof of the Palace of Justice. Once the attack succeeded and was announced as an Ortodoxos uprising, Castro expected other Cubans to support them.

A confident Castro told his followers, "In a few hours you will be victorious or defeated, but regardless of the outcome, . . . this movement will triumph. If you win tomorrow, the aspirations of Martí will be fulfilled sooner. If the contrary occurs, our actions will set an example for the Cuban people."

At 5:00 A.M., the revolutionaries set out in 26 cars. At the gate, someone in the lead car yelled, "Attention, attention, the general is coming." Thinking a military band had arrived for the carnival, the guards presented arms. The rebels disarmed them, but not before the guards sounded an alarm. After that, the Moncada attack was a catastrophe.

Castro had not planned on added patrols. He had not planned on soldiers returning to the barracks in the morning hours. Having placed no one inside the garrison to scout its layout, he sent his "Fidelistas" toward a barbershop instead of the armory. Worst of all, Castro never knew that the rebels with the heaviest firepower had become lost on Santiago's twisting streets.

With Raúl's group firing from the roof, some Fidelistas entered the barracks. They were cut down, their weapons no match for the soldiers' firepower. Santamaria's 24 men captured the hospital, but could not see disaster unfolding. Castro, realizing the hopelessness of the situation, ordered a retreat.

Bullet holes left pocks in the walls of the Moncada army barracks in Santiago, Cuba. Fidel Castro led an unsuccessful attack on the barracks in July 1953. Government forces captured and killed several rebels, and Castro was arrested in August.

Estimates of the numbers of Moncada participants vary. Between 87 and 165 Fidelistas attacked; 262 to 1,000 soldiers fought back. Regardless of the precise numbers, the mission was clearly suicidal. Seeing Castro retreat, Raúl's group escaped, driving by car to the coast. Santamaria's snipers were captured and many were brutally murdered. Only about 60 men returned safely to a farmhouse hideout. Castro set out on foot to the Gran Piedra Sierra mountains with 18 of his men. Peasants along the way fed them roasted pig, tended their wounds, and gave them clothes. Thirty-two other rebels surrendered on July 28, under a guarantee of safekeeping. The next day, Raúl Castro was arrested as he headed toward his parents' home.

On August 1, Lieutenant Pedro Manuel Sarria's 16-man patrol found Castro and his men asleep in a peasant's hut. Sarria cautioned Castro not to identify himself or speak. When one of the soldiers called Castro an assassin, he responded: "It is you who are assassins. . . . It is you who kill unarmed prisoners. . . . You are soldiers of a tyrant!" Despite this violent outburst, Sarria would not permit the soldiers to kill the Fidelistas. Castro was puzzled by Sarria's protection. "Why didn't you kill me?" he asked. "You would have received a nice promotion." Sarria replied, "Muchacho, I am not that kind of man."

Shortly afterward, an army major and his soldiers tried to take the prisoners from Sarria. Sure that the prisoners would be killed, Sarria refused. Bypassing the Macada Prison, he delivered Castro and his men uninjured, with witnesses watching, to the Santiago jail. Thus, Sarria prevented the authorities from torturing the men.

Castro acted more like an honored guest than a prisoner. His interrogation became a speech instead of a confession. His questioner, Colonel Alberto del Rio Chaviano, permitted journalists to interview Castro. He even suggested that Castro tell his story on the radio. "Imagine the imbecility of these people," Castro said. "They ask me to take the micro-phone and to defend my viewpoint before them." Castro gladly complied. In the broadcast, Castro told the listeners, "We came to regenerate Cuba."

History was made on September 21, 1953. Castro turned his trial into a showcase for the rebel cause and its politics. He readily admitted his involvement in the attack, providing details to the judges, journalists, and spectators in the crowded courtroom. He denied collaborating with the Communist or Ortodoxos parties. He told the courtroom he had not worked within the legal system "because since the March 10 coup, one cannot speak. I tell you that we made attempts, but the government, intransigent as ever, did not want to give in."

Castro represented himself and his men, dramatically alternating between the black robes of an attorney and the civilian clothes of a prisoner. He turned their defense into an accusation against Batista, forcing witnesses to describe his revenge on the revolutionaries. Batista had ordered ten rebels killed for every soldier who died. His men delighted in the order. They shot a rebel doctor at point-blank range. One man was beaten to death with rifle butts. Another was thrown against a wall until he died. Still another, wounded in the abdomen, was kicked until he simply split open. A soldier named "*El Tigre*" brought Santamaria's eye to the rebel's sister, demanding that she talk or her brother would lose the other one. She answered, "If he did not tell you under torture, far less will I tell you." Marta Rojas, a young journalist, took notes about the proceedings and smuggled them out in her clothes. People were shocked by the atrocities that were described.

On October 5, 1953, Raúl and two other Fidelistas were sentenced to 13 years in prison. Twenty men received ten-year sentences, and three rebels got three years. Haydee and the other women rebels received sentences of seven months.

Castro's turn came 11 days later under heavy secrecy. In his testimony, Castro explained his political beliefs and detailed Cuba's human suffering. He talked about the Moncada movement and its failure. He condemned Batista in Latin, calling him "*Monstrum Horrendum!*" He paid tribute to the Cuban hero Jose Martí, linking the Moncada attack to duty rather than rebellion. Castro's two-hour oration was later called his "History Will Absolve Me" speech.

The speech was not organized enough to be labeled Marxist, but Castro's emotions and eloquence mesmerized listeners. "I was simply carried by his words," Marta Rojas said. "The same was true with the guards . . . standing with their weapons loose. . . . They were simply absorbed and engrossed by his words."

The speech, which Rojas wrote down, appealed to young idealists. "We were all fascinated," said Vilma Espin, a Castro supporter. "It spoke a new language, and it set out a clear program around which we could all center our struggle."

Castro was sentenced to 15 years in Boniato Prison on the Isle of Pines. Sent 60 miles (97 kilometers) off the coast, he was isolated from events within Cuba. He arrived on Sunday, October 17, 1953, to a depressing prospect of languishing in jail while others furthered his cause.

Castro's incredible ability to turn a catastrophe into an asset soon prevailed, however. In prison, he set up the Abel Santamaria Academy for classes in history, literature, geography, and mathematics. He urged his fellow prisoners to use their time to improve themselves.

Castro himself delved into books. "It seems incredible, hours fly by as if they were minutes, and I, with my restless temperament, spend the day reading, barely moving for anything," he wrote his brother Ramón.

Castro printed out "History Will Absolve Me" with lime juice between the lines of letters. His wife visited him twice a week, delivering Castro's correspondence to Fidelistas who

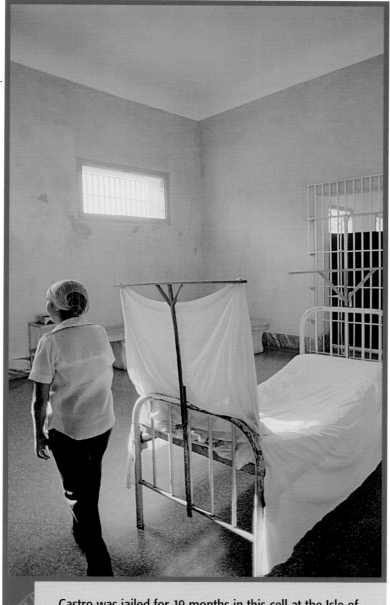

Castro was jailed for 19 months in this cell at the Isle of Pines, off the coast of Cuba. While in prison, he set up an academy with classes in history, literature, geography, and mathematics.

retrieved the "invisible" words by ironing the paper. Castro wanted 100,000 copies of the speech made. His followers' complaints about this impossibility did not sway him.

"What is the difference between 25 and 100,000, only paper and ink," he chided them. With difficulty, they finagled 10,000 copies for distribution.

In February 1954, Castro's marriage unraveled. Perhaps purposefully, he wrote letters to his wife, Mirta, and to his mistress, Naty, on the same day. The letters were somehow switched, and Mirta found out about his affair. Five months later, Castro discovered Mirta's monthly "botella" of $90 to $100 for a nonexistent government job. The media exposed her meager, but illegal, income after Castro insisted that she speak out against the government. For Castro, her employment in Batista's despicable administration was unforgivable. The two later divorced.

On the anniversary of the 26th of July Movement, the minister of the interior and two other officials visited Castro, hinting that a change in his thinking might produce amnesty. Castro replied, "One thousand years in prison before I renounce any of my principles."

Castro's release came long before that. To legitimize his presidency, Batista scheduled elections. The man he had deposed, Grau San Martin, opposed him. For a time, Grau genuinely campaigned, promising to free political prisoners. Batista reluctantly matched the offer. Realizing that the elections were rigged, Grau withdrew. Batista, the newly "elected" president, had to honor his promise. Castro and his men were freed on May 15, 1955.

Castro returned to Havana, holding news conferences and signing autographs. Within ten days, Castro was talking on the radio and giving speeches, attacking Batista. Batista decreed that Castro could not do either. Castro turned instead to magazines, attacking Batista in print. Batista then barred Castro from publishing. His police closed down the magazine the next day. Raúl was charged with setting off a bomb near a movie theater. He eluded the police, sought sanctuary in the Mexican Embassy, and left the country. Convinced that his life was in danger, Castro slipped out of Cuba on July 7 on a tourist visa to Mexico.

6

Revolution Grows in the Mountains

fter the disastrous *Granma* landing in late 1956, the few survivors of Fidel Castro's grand revolutionary army made their way toward the Sierra Maestra mountains.

A struggle could not have begun under worse circumstances, Castro later recalled. "We must say we did not know even one peasant . . . and that the only ideas we had about the Sierra Maestra were those we had studied in the geography books."

Still, Castro had chosen the best place in Cuba to hide from his enemies. The mountain range was 100 miles (161 kilometers) long and nearly 30 miles (48 kilometers) wide. Its terrain was among the most rugged in Cuba. The heat was intolerable and the cold unbearable. Travel was difficult, either on foot or horseback over narrow paths. Though Castro knew nothing of the mountains where he and his men now hid, he soon learned. "In six months, Fidel knew the

Fidel Castro at a rebel camp in the mountains of eastern Cuba in March 1957. After the ill-fated *Granma* landing, Castro and his men hid out in the Sierra Maestra mountains—among the most rugged terrain in Cuba.

Sierra better than I did," Gillermo Garcia later wrote, "and I was born and raised here."

Peasants struggled to survive, growing coffee beans or making charcoal. They were poor, illiterate, and suspicious of anyone in uniform. Castro later recalled that the people could not believe "that a small group of hungry people, ill-clothed, with only a few weapons, could defeat an army that moved on trucks and trains, and in airplanes. . . . The result was that at first we found ourselves in very difficult straits." Castro's scattered revolutionaries arrived at a prearranged rendezvous point on December 16. They rested at the farmhouse of a guerrilla's brother and moved into the Sierra Maestra nine days later.

The peasants, accustomed to the Rural Guard's rough treatment, gradually accepted the rebels. Castro's men did not, as Batista's did, help themselves to the peasants' food, clothing, and women. The peasants liked them even better when Castro told the people that the land would be theirs after the revolution.

Castro's tiny army and its arsenal began to grow. Members of the 26th of July Movement in the city smuggled a small number of guns and ammunition past Batista's men and roadblocks. One woman hid submachine-gun bullets and nine dynamite cartridges under her skirt. Another arrived with three dynamite cartridges and eight hand grenades. Some brought history and geography books to teach the peasant volunteers. By New Year's Eve, 1956, Castro commanded 29 people.

The guerrillas marched deeper into the Sierra Maestra, traveling in the cold rain through heavily wooded areas. Mountain life was not for the unfit or romantic. Castro and his guerrillas slept on the ground or in the mud, drenched by heavy rains. Their uniforms were always mud-streaked and stained with sweat. Their body odor was stifling because they did not bathe. They didn't shave, either; their unkempt beards earned them the nickname "*barbudos*," or "bearded."

The guerrillas moved constantly, changing camps and marching over nearly impassable terrain. Castro's stamina earned him the nickname "*el Caballo*," or "the horse." He lectured his men long after midnight and then would announce, "Well, only 3 A.M. We still have time to walk to the next mountain." Despite the hardships, Castro's little army grew.

Batista, through the media, told the people that Castro had been killed in the *Granma* fighting and diverted their attention to Cuba's prosperity. He also announced the purchase of 16 new B-26 bombers from the United States. Newspapers reported gains in sugar sales and sugar workers' wages, American tourism, and private investments.

Castro needed to prove that he and his cause were still alive. He attacked La Plata's barracks on January 16. After an hour of heavy fighting, the 11-man garrison surrendered. The guerrillas took nine Springfield rifles, one Thompson submachine gun, and 10,000 rounds of ammunition. They set fire to the barracks, treated the five wounded soldiers, released them, and simply disappeared.

The battle sent Batista a clear message: The revolution still survived. It also established Castro's code of justice. The rebels did not purchase weapons; they captured them. They didn't torture or execute their enemies; they freed them. "Only cowards and thugs murder an enemy when he has surrendered," Castro told his men. "The rebel army cannot carry out the same tactics as the tyranny which we fight." In camp, Castro insisted that his men pay for anything supplied by the peasants. They cared for civilians who were harmed for helping them, though they executed anyone suspected of murder, rape, or betrayal.

Weary of the Rural Guard's brutalities, more peasants embraced Castro's cause. Those too young or too inexperienced were put into paramilitary groups as spies. "We always know where the soldiers are," Castro later told journalists. "But they never know where we are."

Once, Batista's forces did learn the location of Castro's camp. Having survived the *Granma* landing and the sugar-cane ambush, the rebels were betrayed by a peasant guide. After being captured and threatened with execution, Eutimio Guerra agreed to assassinate Castro and pinpoint the rebels' location for Batista's B-26 bombers. He actually slept beside

Castro on one occasion, but lacked the nerve to use his gun against his leader. Guerra's suspicious behavior and his many questions persuaded Castro to move the rebel camp 300 yards (274 meters) up the mountainside. If he had not, the guerrillas would have been obliterated by the January 28 bombing. Under attack, the rebels split into three groups, led by Castro and his chief aides, Raúl and Che Guevara. Strafed by airplanes and chased by Batista soldiers, they fled west toward a safe house, eating nothing and drinking little for two days.

Eighteen days later, they arrived for a scheduled meeting with the movement's National Directorate, which led the urban underground and supported Castro's guerrilla warfare in the Sierra Maestra. Castro was also to meet two people who would change his life and the revolution. The first, Celia Sanchez Manduley, was a dedicated member of the 26th of July Movement when she and Castro met that day. She worked with the underground network that brought food and arms to the guerrillas. She had been among those waiting for the *Granma*'s landing the previous December. The chemistry between leader and follower was instant. For the next 23 years, she would arrange his notes, find his pens, schedule his dental appointments, and reprimand his stubbornness. She had organized a meeting with a *New York Times* correspondent, the second great influence on Castro and his cause.

Herbert Matthews was a good candidate to break through Batista's censorship and relay Castro's message to the Cuban people and the world. He was a respected authority on Latin America and was conveniently vacationing in Cuba. The journalist traveled six hours by jeep and two hours on foot to meet Castro. They talked for three hours in whispers.

Matthews later wrote, "The personality of the man is overpowering. It is easy to see . . . why he has caught the imagination of the youth of Cuba. . . . Here was an educated, dedicated fanatic, a man of ideals, of courage, and of remarkable qualities of leadership."

Matthews's three-part article first appeared on February 24, 1957. It told the world that Castro was very much alive. It artfully described Castro's ideas about government, and it verified people's growing opposition to Batista's regime. Matthews wrote, "President Fulgencio Batista has the cream of his army around the area, but the army men are fighting a thus-far losing battle to destroy the most dangerous enemy General Batista has yet faced. . . ."

Castro reassured the American newspaperman that the rebels were only fighting for an end to Batista's dictatorship and for a democratic Cuba, saying, "You can be sure we have no animosity toward the United States and the American people." His statement would later be proven false.

Despite Matthews's descriptive and analytical powers, he was completely fooled by a carefully planned masquerade. As Castro and Matthews talked, Castro's 18 soldiers took turns walking near the newsman. One, whose only shirt had no back, always approached Matthews from the front. Thus, Matthews counted 45 men in the clearing. Another interrupted the interview with "information" from Castro's other positions. The journalist concluded that many more troops waited elsewhere.

Matthews's article outraged Batista. He challenged the newsman's credibility. He did not believe anyone could slip into the Sierra Maestra unnoticed by his military. *The Times* then published photographs of Matthews with Castro. The pictures transported Castro out of the mountain mists and onto the world stage. Now a Cuban hero and an international celebrity, Castro healed a century-old wound in Cuba's national psyche. For once, the world acknowledged and respected a Cuban.

Castro and his mountain revolutionaries were not the only ones who opposed the Batista regime. A university

Robert Taber of CBS News interviews Fidel Castro in his secret mountain stronghold in November 1957. The interview was shown in the CBS News report *Rebels of the Sierra Maestra*.

group tried to assassinate Batista. Castro would not have supported the plan had he known about it. He proclaimed, "I am against terrorism. I condemn these procedures. Nothing is solved by them. Here in the Sierra Maestra is where they should come to fight." Other rebel groups existed throughout the country. They all wanted to depose Batista, but they did not agree about how to do it. The same proved true for Castro's 26th of July Movement. Its urban arm kept the administration off balance with bombings and organized strikes. It also supplied Castro with arms and volunteers. However, it did not like Castro's rule-by-personality style. It favored a more sedate, govern-by-committee approach to forming policy. Its new plan, which Castro rejected, would have given the guerrillas just one vote among several.

By May 25, 1957, the rebels were more organized. A courier system, counterintelligence, and food drops were established among the peasants. Recruits, sent by the urban underground into the mountains, boosted the army to 120 men. Castro planned an attack outside the Sierra Maestra on a 50-man garrison located 25 miles (40 kilometers) east of La Plata. The Fidelistas defeated Batista's men in 20 minutes. The so-called El Uvero victory proved be a turning point for them. Che Guevara wrote, "[O]ur guerrillas had reached full maturity. From that moment, our morale increased enormously."

Meanwhile, the morale of Batista's soldiers plummeted. Ordinary soldiers who sympathized with the 26th of July Movement planned to overtake four garrisons throughout Cuba. Batista crushed the uprising with a bloodbath of his own soldiers. His viciousness turned other government soldiers toward Castro's cause. Yet, the United States continued to back Batista.

In September 1957, Castro's guerrillas increased their offensive. They set their first deliberate trap for government troops, ambushing them near Pino del Agua. In November, Castro ordered the guerrillas to burn 6.5 million tons of Cuba's sugarcane, valued at half a billion dollars. One of the first plantations burned was his own family's farm. His mother never forgave him.

Throughout 1957 Castro enlarged his "Free Territory" in the Oriente Province. Guevara was given the title of commandant (major) and sent to the southeast. He excelled in organization, and soon his camp looked like a small town, complete with a hospital, a prison, a school, and a newspaper. In March 1958, Raúl was given command of a second front in the Sierra Cristal mountains west of the Sierra Maestra.

The United States walked a double line with the Batista regime. On March 14, 1958, Washington, D.C., announced that it would no longer send arms to Cuba because Batista had used American arms in Cuba's internal conflicts instead of protecting the Western Hemisphere. On the other hand, Washington did not openly support Castro. U.S. President Dwight D. Eisenhower was suspicious of rebellions and revolutionaries.

With Castro's consent, the urban section of the 26th of July Movement planned a nationwide strike to bring down Batista. The April 9 event turned out to be a catastrophe. The group's various factions quarreled among themselves, and the organizers kept the actual date secret, expecting Cubans to strike immediately when the radio announced it. The announcement was broadcast at midday, when most workers were at their jobs.

With the strike's failure, Castro had had enough. During a May 3 meeting with the Havana and Santiago leaders, Castro took complete control of the movement. He became the commander-in-chief of the underground militias as well as of his Sierra men. He also became secretary-general, assuming political leadership of the entire organization.

Thinking that the strike's failure showed a weakening among the rebels, Batista ordered 10,000 men into the Oriente Province to isolate the Sierra Maestra. The sheer numbers of his army should have crushed Castro's forces, but the rebels knew where to hide and escaped without serious injuries. Planes, supplied by the United States and refueled at Guantánamo Bay, inflicted terrible casualties on civilians instead.

Castro's letter to Celia Sanchez on June 5, 1958, held an ominous prediction: "I've sworn that the Americans are going to pay dearly for what they are doing. When this war is over, a much wider and bigger war will begin for me, the war I am going to wage against them."

Castro was not so decisive about his stand on the Cuban Communists. The Castro of the mountains and the Communist Party circled each other warily. The Communists distrusted

Castro's action-oriented personality. He realized that the party's 17,000 members were too important to ignore. Yet, he thought the Communists were far too structured and too tightly tied to the Soviet Union. Associating with either would have killed the 26th of July Movement. Rumors implying that Castro was a Communist infuriated him. "I hate Soviet imperialism as much as I hate Yankee [American] imperialists," he said. "I am not breaking my neck fighting one dictatorship to fall into another." Castro's 26th of July Movement met with eight other revolutionary groups in Caracas, Venezuela, in a show of unity. When the Caracas Pact was signed on July 20, the Communists were conspicuously absent. Actually, Castro's real allegiance rested in a party based on his own principles.

In November, Castro named Manuel Urrutia Lleo as the provisional government president. This achieved several objectives. Appointing the judge who sided with him during the Moncada trials defused the tension between the mountain fighters and their city counterparts. It blocked opposition leaders and former President Prio from assuming the presidency once Batista fell. And Urrutia's appointment gave the Fidelistas a representative who could talk with foreign officials, especially in Washington.

Batista's last hurrah lasted through 30 clashes over 76 days. Castro's men fired down on the army from positions high on the crest of the mountains. Other rebels drove back an offensive up the La Plata River, taking 220 prisoners. Their repeated victories and the approaching rainy season demoralized Batista's army. It pulled out on August 7, 1958. Cuba was Castro's for the taking.

Just as landing a boat on the Oriente Province replicated Martí's invasion in 1895, Castro planned his final offensive from the past. He modeled his three-part plan after one used in the 1851 War of Independence. Castro and Raúl remained in Oriente Province to capture Santiago. Castro sent Camilo

Castro reads a newspaper while at his rebel base in 1957. Throughout that year, Castro expanded his control over territory in the Oriente Province.

Cienfuegos north to Pinar del Rio on Cuba's eastern edge. Guevara was to take control of two rival Directorate groups and one supported by former President Prio. All three operated in the Escambray Mountains. Guevara's military mission was the most dangerous. His men marched for six weeks through salt swamps. They traveled barefoot, their feet too swollen to fit into boots. Near starvation, they ate parts of palm trees and raw horseflesh to survive. Yet, they cut the country in half by capturing Cuba's roads, railroads, and communications. Guevara captured 400 soldiers and a million rounds of ammunition, essentially ending the war.

By December, U.S. officials realized that Batista's days were numbered. They tried to get him to resign so the presidency could be filled before Castro reached Havana. Batista resisted, however, claiming victory was near. All the time, Castro gained power as the people and Batista's soldiers joined him. The rebels attacked Santa Clara on December 18. With his last stronghold gone, Batista bowed to the inevitable.

At 3:00 A.M. on New Year's Day, 1959, Batista left Cuba for good. Students draped buildings in the red and black flags of the 26th of July Movement. In Havana, people cried with joy.

7

The
Triumphal
Entry

When Batista fled Cuba early on New Year's Day, 1959, he left behind an army of 40,000 soldiers and 15,000 new recruits. They had outnumbered their guerrilla conquerors ten to one.

Cubans turned their liberation into a festival and then into a riot. They spilled out into the streets, honking car horns, hugging each other, and dancing. The carnival-like atmosphere then turned ugly. Encouraged by thugs, the crowd transformed into a mob. It surged about, destroying parking meters and casinos.

Castro ordered Guevara and Cienfuegos to Havana. They quickly restored order, controlling Havana's radio, television, and airport. They reclaimed the police stations and government buildings, they arrested police and ex-Batista officials, and they released political prisoners jailed by Batista. Journalist Edwin Tetlo said,

Rebel soldiers line a roadway on January 7, 1959. After President Fulgencio Batista fled Cuba on January 1, Castro traveled across the country from Santiago to Havana and was met by crowds of adoring people.

"They were too good to be real. . . . To a man they behaved impeccably."

Meanwhile, Castro took Santiago without firing a single shot. He spoke at the Moncada barracks, where the revolution had begun. He was greeted by 163,000 people. "This time, luckily for Cuba, the revolution will truly come into power," he told the crowd. "It will not be like 1898, when the North Americans came and made themselves masters of our country. . . . For the first time the republic will really be entirely free and the people will have what they deserve. . . . This war was won by the people!"

On January 3, Castro left Santiago for Havana. The long and winding trip was a 600-mile (966-kilometer) hug. The people wanted to touch him, embrace him, and talk with him. His comrade, Raúl Chibas, later wrote, "Every five minutes, at every intersection of the highway, women stopped him; the old women kissed him, telling him he was greater than Jesus Christ."

Castro was in no hurry to enter Havana; he wanted people to connect with him. He listened to pleas for housing projects, hospitals, medicine, and schools. He visited the mother of a slain soldier. He conducted interviews with U.S. journalists, including the television celebrity Ed Sullivan. Wherever he stopped, radio and television crews covered his speeches. Guevara and Cienfuegos had secured the capital. Raúl Castro stayed in Santiago as the Oriente's military governor. A thousand rebels trailed down the Central Highway, where admirers joined in the march.

On January 7, the United States officially recognized Castro's new revolutionary government. The next day, Castro entered Havana on a tank with his son, Fidelito, beside him. Bells rang, whistles and sirens blew, cannons fired. He stopped to see the *Granma* anchored in the harbor before proceeding to the Presidential Palace. More than a million cheering people crowded around him. A rifle slung over his shoulder, Castro greeted his chosen provisional president and gave a short speech. One story recounts that Castro, unable to move through the crowd, raised his arm and asked the people to let him pass. Instantly, the crowd parted. A journalist wrote, "I have never seen such respect and awe." A U.S. Embassy officer put it another way. "That guy knew how to press the button," he said.

En route to Havana, Castro had announced his next plan of action. "We are going to purify this country," he declared. Few realized what he meant.

His purifications began when he faced down his last military opponent, the Revolutionary Student Directorate, which broke into the garrison, taking weapons and ammunition. Without naming the Directorate in his first political speech, he asked his audience why anyone needed arms: "What are these arms for? Against whom are they going to be used? Against the revolutionary government that has the support of the whole people?" The crowd responded, "No!" He asked again, "Are we going to take up arms against a free government that respects the rights of the people?" Again, the crowd yelled, "No!" The Directorate soon returned the munitions.

Dialoguing with the crowd became one of Castro's favorite practices. Later, in this "direct democracy," he would question his audience about a controversial problem so that the people could appear to be directing his actions.

As he addressed Havana's jubilant citizens, a white dove, Cuba's symbol of life, landed on his shoulder; others hovered nearby. Calm fell over the masses. Former soldiers removed their caps and put their hands over their hearts. Others fell to their knees in prayer. The Castro myth immediately rose to the level of the religious. Cuba's bigger-than-life hero seemed heaven-sent.

Castro's next purifications concerned the Batista assassins and torturers who had terrorized the country. About 20,000 people were arrested, tried, and then executed. Raúl Castro tried 70 together, bulldozing their bodies into a common grave. The trial of Major Jesus Sosa Blanco, a well-known Batista administration murderer, was conducted in the Sports Palace, where a mob of 17,000 people yelled taunts at the defendant while peanuts and ice cream were sold in the stands. Though Castro intended the exhibition to demonstrate the trials' fairness, the world was appalled by the spectacle.

"The North Americans have never shown a moral disgust

Hundreds of thousands of people gathered in the park in front of the Presidential Palace in Havana in January 1959 to hear Castro speak. One journalist wrote, "I have never seen such respect and awe."

of Batista's crimes," Castro countered. "What was done at Hiroshima and Nagasaki? . . . We have shot no child, we have shot no woman, we have shot no old people. . . . We are shooting the assassins."

Cuba's new commander-in-chief claimed to have no political ambitions. "I am a soldier in the ranks," Castro insisted. "No act of ours will ever interfere with or detract one iota from the authority of the president." Yet, during the first month after his triumphal entry, he gave 12 speeches, held five news conferences, and appeared twice on television. He made laws that President Urrutia merely signed. While Urrutia appointed respected experts to the cabinet to study Cuba's complex problems, Castro proclaimed that unemployment would disappear and that Cuba's standard of living would exceed the United States' and the Soviet Union's.

His unofficial government began purifying the old society to make way for a new one, based on Marxist-Leninist socialism. Just six weeks after the new government's creation, the prime minister resigned. Castro assumed the post. Then, Castro disregarded the judicial system. When 40 Batista air force pilots, bombardiers, and mechanics were acquitted of bombing civilians, he ordered a new trial. The court got the message. In the second trial, the men received lengthy prison terms.

Although Castro had masterminded a revolution in the mountains, he was unprepared for the details of governing, the mounds of paperwork, and the consequences of his decisions. Running a government, even unofficially, was very complex. He compared his struggles to his *Granma* landing: "The more problems we solve, the more problems appear."

Herbert Matthews, the *New York Times* correspondent, agreed. Castro was "too untrained, inexpert, and impractical to grasp what has to be done and how to do it," he wrote.

However, Castro did grasp how quietly and slowly he had to work to include the Cuban Communists in the new government he planned. The 26th of July Movement and the Communists had always distrusted each other. With the Cold War between the United States and the Soviet Union, America would not tolerate any Communist influence in a government so close to its shores. So Castro, his aides, and the Communist leadership met secretly. They established Revolutionary Instruction Schools to teach Marxism-Leninism to promising young Fidelistas. They merged Communist groups into one party.

Castro's most important purification concerned the influence of the United States. Cuba's economy was a complex tangle, all of which led back to the United States. On the surface, Cuba was a prosperous Latin American nation. Its per capita income of 367 pesos was three times higher than that of other Latino countries. Yet U.S. businesses controlled 40 percent of Cuba's sugar production. Americans owned the largest and most efficient sugar mills, 80 percent of Cuba's public utilities, 90 percent of its mineral wealth, and (along with Great Britain) most of the oil and gas. Former U.S. Ambassador Earl E.T. Smith told a Senate subcommittee that "the American ambassador was the second most important man in Cuba, sometimes even more important than the president."

He was also the most despised. Cubans blamed injustice and inequality in their country on the U.S. presence. Seventy-five percent of the agricultural land was owned by only 8 percent of the property holders. The rest of Cuba's people were shamefully poor and illiterate. A million women and children had never worn shoes. Consequently, 95 percent had intestinal parasites. Half a million Cubans never tasted milk or meat after infancy. Of more than 1.5 million people who worked in 1957, nearly a million earned the equivalent of $75 a month. Cubans wanted foreigners out Cuba. Now free of Batista, they wanted their country back. They looked to Castro to free them again.

Within a month of taking Havana, Castro was in Venezuela seeking a pact with the Venezuelans against the United States. He also asked for Venezuelan oil and a loan of $300 million, two things that would help loosen the United States' grip on Cuba. The Venezuelan president declined his requests.

In February 1959, the American Society of Newspaper Editors invited Castro to speak at its April 17 meeting in Washington. He accepted, seeing the 11 days in the United States (and four more in Canada and Argentina), as an opportunity to introduce other countries to the new Cuba.

His visit was a public relations triumph. A thousand Cubans met him at the airport. In New York and Washington, crowds lined the streets to see this revolutionary hero. University students at Harvard and Princeton gave him standing ovations and carried him on their shoulders, and 30,000 people came to New York's Central Park for a nighttime speech. "We have never met Americans like these," Castro proclaimed.

His speech before the 1,000 newspaper editors lasted more than two hours. He reassured his audience that Cuba would not seize foreign land or industry and that the U.S. naval base would remain at Guantánamo Bay. He described his revolution as "humanist." He stressed creating new industry in Cuba. "We did not come here for money," he said.

The trip was a disaster for the changing United States–Cuban relationship, though. To avoid meeting this not-quite-ordinary Cuban citizen but not-quite national head of state, President Eisenhower scheduled a golf trip to Georgia. In his place, Vice President Richard M. Nixon spoke with Castro for two hours. Nixon did not treat Castro as a bona fide head of state. Instead, he lectured the Cuban leader about the recent public executions, the lack of free elections, and Castro's seeming reliance on the people to make government policy.

Castro at a meeting of the American Society of Newspaper Editors in Washington, D.C., on April 17, 1959. Castro scored some public relations victories with his visit, but U.S. President Dwight D. Eisenhower scheduled a trip to avoid meeting Castro.

In a long memo to Eisenhower, Nixon described Castro as an "idealistic and impractical young man." The vice president suggested that "he is either incredibly naive about Communism or under Communist discipline. My guess is the former." Nixon also recommended implementing a covert operation to overthrow him. Eighteen years later, Castro told TV journalist Barbara Walters, "Sincerely, I never liked Richard Nixon. From the first moment, I could see he was a false man. He always hated our country."

Other conversations with the Eisenhower administration kept Castro on the defensive. U.S. officials were horrified at Cuba's "war crimes" trials. They also worried about the many Communists around Castro.

"Wherever we go, people are asking questions about what we are," Castro later complained to a Cuban magazine editor. "You know we are socialists, but the Americans are so confused. If I say 'socialist,' they believe you are a 'Communist.' "

After stops in Canada and Argentina, Castro returned home and unveiled his new land-reform program. On May 17, 1959, he signed the new reform law in La Plata, the site of his guerrilla headquarters. The law limited individual landholdings to 1,000 acres (405 hectares). Rice, cattle, and sugar holdings were limited to 3,300 acres (1,336 hectares). Properties exceeding these limits were broken up into 67-acre (27-hectare) parcels. Though 200,000 peasants received land this way, they could not sell or mortgage their new land, and they had to deliver crops at a price set by the newly created National Institute of Agrarian Reform (INRA). Foreigners could own sugar mills and large tracts of land, with government permission. They could not acquire new land, however. Castro's program threw U.S.-Cuban relations in the wastebasket.

Castro later admitted, "It truly established a rupture between the revolution and the richest and the most privileged sectors in the country, and a rupture with the United States." He was right. Large American businesses owned huge amounts of Cuban land.

Within the INRA, Castro created another government cabinet. It included the departments of industrialization, banking, commercialization, and transportation, which was

Castro, at a meeting in June 1959, with Captain Antonio Nuñez Jimenez, left, director of the National Institute of Agrarian Reform, and Oscar Pino Santos, right, an economist. The institute, under land-reform laws signed the month before, would dictate owner-ship and use of all Cuban land.

responsible for highways, peasant housing, and tourist resorts. The INRA also had a 100,000-man army.

With the real power in the INRA's infrastructure, Castro eliminated Cuba's president. Urrutia had done everything Castro asked, but, like others, he was critical of the increasing Communist influence in Cuba. Castro's plan began with the July 17 edition of the *Revolución*. In it, he announced his resignation as prime minister. That evening, Castro attacked Urrutia on television. He said Urrutia's concerns that the government was Communist "bordered on treason." He said Urrutia's cabinet had not produced significant reform. He complained that he was kept busy traveling to the United States, Canada, and Argentina, and that news conferences, meetings, and speeches left no time for his duties. He said that Urrutia delayed signing legislation and that Urrutia paid himself the same salary Batista had. Castro said Cuba had to choose: either the president or himself.

Predictably, thousands took to the streets, clamoring for Castro's return and Urrutia's resignation. Before the evening was over, Urrutia resigned. He fled to the Venezuelan Embassy disguised as a milkman.

Che Guevara described the bond between Castro and his people as "the dialogue of two tuning forks whose vibrations summon forth vibrations in each other." Castro announced that he would let the people decide his political future at a mass rally on July 26, the sixth anniversary of the Moncada uprising. Then, the newly sworn-in (more flexible and more Communist) president, Osvaldo Dorticos, announced that Castro "bowed" to the people's wish that he return. The people were deliriously happy. For the millions who gathered at his mass rallies, Castro was everything. His picture was everywhere, including in a nativity scene as one of the three wise men. Children learned their alphabet by saying "F is for Castro."

Through July and August, newspapers, loyal aides, and the United States grew more concerned about the Communist presence around Castro. One conservative newspaper compared the Fidelistas to watermelons—"green on the outside [their uniform color] and red [symbolic of communism] on the inside."

Huber Matos, a respected Fidelista, resigned as commandant of the Camaguey Province and expressed his anti-Communist feelings in a letter to Castro. By now, Castro believed that any anti-Communist statement was an antirevolutionary statement, and decided to purify the situation. Overlooking Matos's past loyalties, Castro personally arrested him in October 1959. He accused Matos, like Urrutia, of treason.

Just as his trial was under way, a B-25 flew over the capital, dropping anti-Communist materials. The pamphlets, signed by the pilot, Diaz Lanz, urged Castro to eliminate communism. Antiaircraft weapons and Cuban planes tried unsuccessfully to shoot Lanz down. Two civilians were killed, and several were wounded. Castro used the incident to accuse the United States of bombing Havana. He whipped up the crowds, asking, "What reason do they have for attacking Cuba?" The futures of Matos and the United States–Cuban relationship were doomed.

Castro, in a long speech before 400,000 people, lumped the newspaper criticisms, Matos's resignation, and the civilian deaths into one conspiracy. He handpicked the judges, prosecutor, and witnesses at Matos's trial. He himself "testified" for seven and a half hours. Matos was sentenced to 20 years in prison. His trial was the first of many that dealt unfairly with "counter-revolutionaries" as more antigovernment and anti-Castro groups began to organize throughout Cuba.

Castro's speech on October 26 effectively ended efforts by the United States to resolve the tension between the two countries. The U.S. ambassador sent a letter saying such charges were "inaccurate," "malicious," and "misleading," and accused Cuba of wanting to "replace traditional friendship with enmity." Two days later, at a news conference, President Eisenhower puzzled "why the Cubans would now be, and the Cuban government would be, so unhappy, when, after all, their principal market is right here."

Shortly afterward, the Central Intelligence Agency (CIA) began to plan an overthrow of Castro. The project would turn into the Bay of Pigs invasion.

If Castro wanted alliances for sugar, loans, or arms, he had effectively eliminated the United States as a possibility. The Soviet Union waited in the East, however, eager to gain a toehold in the Western Hemisphere.

8

Barking With the Big Dogs

Fidel Castro continued his turn from West to East. By antagonizing the United States and welcoming the Soviet Union, he caused two events that made "Castro" and "Cuba" household words. The first, the Bay of Pigs invasion, ended in a humiliating defeat for the United States. The second, the Cuban Missile Crisis, pitted superpower against superpower in a confrontation so dangerous that the entire world gasped.

Castro's crusade against the United States sliced into American companies and investors. The Agrarian Land Reform Bill had authorized the seizure of American properties, buildings, equipment, and livestock. He seized U.S.-owned large sugar plantations, cattle ranches, sugar mills, and utility companies.

Support from the Soviet Union gave Castro more freedom to attack the United States. On February 4, 1960, Anastas Mikoyan, the

A representation of Fidel Castro at the famous Prado in Havana in April 1960. The sign reads, "Fidel, giant guide of America."

Soviet first deputy premier, praised Castro's agrarian-reform program and signed an economic pact with Cuba. The Soviets agreed to buy 425,000 tons of sugar in 1960 and a million tons in each of the next four years. They agreed to loans of $100 million for the next 12 years. They would supply oil, fertilizer, steel, and iron. Soviet technicians would build new factories, filling the vacuum left by Cuban professionals who defected to the United States.

In his speeches, Castro stirred up Cubans' long-simmering fears of an American invasion: The United States wanted to control Cuba; the United States wanted to destroy Cuba. On television, he described U.S. "stupidities." He criticized the United States for allowing Cuban exiles to harass him from Florida. In March, when a French ship loaded with 70 tons of Belgian ammunitions mysteriously exploded in Havana Harbor, Castro immediately accused the United States of sabotage.

In May, Castro demanded that American oil companies process Soviet crude oil in their refineries. When they refused, Castro seized them. Shortly after, he took additional American-owned sugar mills and utility companies, costing the United States $850 million. Eisenhower countered by canceling America's remaining sugar purchases. Immediately, the Soviet Union offered to buy any sugar the United States did not. "The U.S.S.R. is raising its voice and extending a helpful hand to the people of Cuba," Soviet Premier Nikita Khrushchev said. "Speaking figuratively, in case of necessity, Soviet artillerymen can support the Cuban people with rocket fire." Castro liked the idea of the Soviets' defending Cuba should the United States attack.

The two men met face-to-face in New York at the United Nations' fifteenth anniversary on September 20, 1960. Castro made headlines by accusing the hotel that the United States provided of overcharging him and by hustling his 80 "barbudos" off to Harlem, among the city's poor. Few people noticed that he had made the reservations the day before. At the General Assembly, Khrushchev made headlines by beating his shoe on the table as another delegate spoke. After Khrushchev drove to Castro's hotel, the two leaders embraced in a bear hug.

When Castro spoke at the United Nations, standing in New York City before world representatives, he criticized the

Soviet Premier Nikita Khrushchev welcomes Castro for dinner on September 23, 1960, at the headquarters of the Soviet UN delegation in New York. The Soviets liked having a comrade in the Western Hemisphere, so close to the United States.

United States and aligned Cuba with the Third World oppressed. After Khrushchev's General Assembly speech, Castro congratulated him before anyone else. The two men embraced again, and the cameras flashed. Castro left New York assured of continued Soviet support. He told the 125,000 people who greeted him in Havana that the United States was a "cold and hostile nation."

The Cuba–United States relationship dissolved. President Eisenhower recalled his ambassador on October 10. The next day, he announced an economic embargo against Cuba. The United States would sell Cuba nothing but food and medical supplies.

Castro counterattacked. Three months later, during the second anniversary celebration of the revolution, Castro told the crowd that the U.S. Embassy's staff must be reduced to match the 11-man Cuban staff in Washington. The crowd yelled, "Get them out of here, throw them out!" The United States broke off diplomatic relations the next day.

President-elect John F. Kennedy learned of secret plans to overthrow Castro shortly after the November 1960 elections. Suggested by Vice President Nixon and approved by President Eisenhower, the plan included air strikes against Castro's air force, a landing of exiled Cubans at the Bay of Pigs, and an uprising of the Cuban people.

Kennedy had talked tough on Cuba during the hard-fought presidential campaign against Nixon. His chief advisors supported the plan. Even so, Kennedy feared negative world opinion if the United States openly supported the anti-Castro rebels, and he did not really commit to the plan.

The invasion at the Bay of Pigs was fatally flawed. First, it was an open secret. So many people knew about the plan that Cuban children actually played a game called "Cuban and Yankee Invaders." *The New York Times* ran a front-page story on January 10, 1961, titled "U.S. Helps Train an Anti-Castro Force at Secret Guatemalan Air-Ground Base." The subheads read, "Clash with Cuba Feared" and "Installations Built with American Aid." Castro himself knew that an invasion was coming, and he was well prepared. He put troops on 24-hour duty. He appealed for donations of blood and food. He detained 35,000 suspected "counterrevolutionaries" in concentration camps. Ironically, shortly before the invasion, he visited the Cienaga de Zapata swamp. Looking at the Bay of Pigs beaches, he said, "This is a great place for a landing. We should place a .50-caliber heavy machine gun there, just in case."

A day before the invasion forces landed at the Bay of Pigs, the second vital element of the plan failed: The invasion depended on the complete destruction of Cuba's air force. Realizing it would be targeted, Castro hid his operational planes days before. On April 15, 1961, six planes, piloted by Cuban exiles, flew toward Havana, Santiago, and San Antonio. They bombed only decoy or broken planes. Eight Cuban planes survived to attack during the Bay of Pigs landing. Alerted to what was coming, Castro put his troops—a 25,000-man army and 200,000 militiamen—on high alert.

Meanwhile, on April 14, the 1,400-man invasion force of CIA-trained soldiers had sailed away from Nicaragua under American escort, with Nicaraguan dictator Anastasio Somoza saying, "Bring me a couple of hairs from Castro's beard!" The CIA planned a quiet, covert landing, which began shortly before midnight on April 16. Instead, the "*brigadistas*" found reefs where the CIA expected seaweed. They found several thousand charcoal workers instead of isolated territory. Further, the CIA had not noticed that the mountains where the rebels were to hide were too far away. Another element of the CIA's plan was a failure.

Castro heard of the invasion about 1:15 A.M. He immediately ordered his forces into the Zapata area and then moved there himself. Castro knew the invasion forces could not unload their equipment or establish a beachhead where a provisional government could be set up. Once the invaders announced a new government, the United States would recognize it, and Castro would be ousted. He personally told his pilot, "I want you to sink those ships!"

The CIA had been so confident in its plan that it had not installed antiaircraft guns on the boats. When the Cuban planes attacked, the boats were helpless. One ran aground; another blew up. The rest fled to the open sea, abandoning the brigadistas. Without reinforcements or ammunition, the invasion was essentially finished.

Castro's 20,000 troops, artillery, and tanks surrounded the brigadistas. The invaders radioed the ships off shore for ammunitions and cover fire. President Kennedy, however, stopped American planes from protecting them. On the afternoon of April 19, the brigadistas' commander ordered them to escape however they could.

The air force pilots, the CIA advisors, and navy personnel stood by helplessly as the brigadistas fought a losing battle. "We were supposed to protect them," one pilot said in frustration. "And yet, they wouldn't let us do it."

About 80 freedom fighters died, and 1,189 brigadistas were captured. Estimates of losses in Castro's forces varied from 87 to 2,000.

Speaking at the funeral of seven who died in the attack, Castro compared the air strike to Pearl Harbor, describing the attack on Cuba as "twice as treacherous and a thousand times more cowardly." He called the U.S. government "liars" for bombarding Cuba's air force and the Soviet Union "admirable" for putting a man in space. He also told the mourners, "What the imperialists cannot forgive us . . . is that we have made a socialist revolution under the noses of the United States." It was the first time he had said the word *socialist* in public.

Castro's televised speech on April 20 established him, the so-called "Maximum Leader," as the conqueror of the mighty United States. Using maps and charts from the captured rebels, he described how he had destroyed the American invasion. He

Two Cuban exiles, captured after the failed Bay of Pigs invasion, walked past Cuban soldiers on April 19, 1961. A force of about 1,400 Cuban exiles, backed by the CIA, landed at the Bay of Pigs on April 17, hoping to spark a popular uprising to oust Fidel Castro. The Cuban military killed or captured most of the exiles.

said, "The imperialist looks at the geography, analyzes the number of cannons, of planes, of tanks. . . . The revolutionary goes to the social population and asks, 'Who are these people?' . . . The revolutionary thinks first of the people. . . .'"

He was right. The project's planners had assumed that Cuba wanted to be saved from Castro, but Castro had returned Cuba to its people. They would never have turned on the man who had given their country back to them. Cubans accepted the food shortages, the ban on the free press, and even Castro's ban on Santa Claus.

On April 21, Castro put groups of prisoners from the failed invasion on television for journalists to question. After four nights, Castro himself interrogated about a thousand prisoners in the Havana Sports Palace. He coaxed them to confess and deflected their accusations about Cuba's democracy. One asked Castro how he would have conducted the invasion. The group even applauded him. Castro laughed as one man said he expected to be executed. Castro said, "This gentleman is the first prisoner in the world who gets a chance to debate the leader of a nation he came to invade."

Vetoing the people's demands for executions, Castro suggested ransoming the men. Though the United States would not negotiate in cash, it did exchange about $48,000 in medicine, goods, and equipment for each man. The total reached $53 million. The American negotiator jokingly suggested that he might defeat Castro in elections after giving Cuba so much equipment and supplies. Castro replied, not so humorously, "I think you may be right, so there will be no elections."

A week later, Castro made good on his statement. In his May Day speech, commemorating a socialist holiday, Castro threw out the constitution's instructions for elections. He said his "direct democracy" with the people made them unnecessary. Cubans hardly noticed.

Castro controlled all of his country and most of his people.

Defeating their northern enemy temporarily distracted them from everyday problems. They did not think about the 3,500 rebels who no longer accepted Castro's government. Hiding in the Escambray Mountains and the Oriente Province, these new revolutionaries cost the government $1 billion in ruined crops, burned houses, and destroyed roads and bridges. The fact that sugar production was down and cattle herds were depleted were not as important to ordinary Cubans as humiliating the United States.

With elections officially eliminated, Castro finally came out and declared that he was a socialist. On December 1, 1961, he told a television audience, "I am a Marxist-Leninist and shall remain a Marxist-Leninist until the day I die."

The statement marked a new influence among Third World countries and in the Western Hemisphere. The Soviets, with their structured organization of a state-run party, were not very enthusiastic about the impetuous, egocentric, unorganized Castro. Still, they liked having a socialist comrade in the Western Hemisphere so close to the United States.

Attorney General Robert Kennedy recognized America's vulnerability. He wrote to his brother, the president: "If we don't want Russia to set up missile bases in Cuba, we had better decide now what we are willing to do to stop it."

After the Bay of Pigs fiasco, the CIA examined ways to eliminate or discredit Castro personally. "Operation Mongoose" considered contaminating his cigars with botulism, dropping cyanide tablets in his milkshakes, and spraying chemicals on his shoes to make his beard fall out. The CIA even contacted the Mafia to find a "contract" expert. Within 18 months, Robert Kennedy's fears were realized in the Cuban Missile Crisis, a six-day incident in which the United States and the Soviet Union veered dangerously close to nuclear war.

After the Bay of Pigs victory, Castro expected an invasion by American troops. "We must prepare ourselves for that direct invasion," he said. He believed Cuba's expulsion from the

Organization of American States (OAS) in January 1962 was a prelude to an attack. He wanted Soviet protection.

Some analysts believe that the idea of placing Soviet missiles in Cuba surfaced in July 1962 during Raúl Castro's visit with Khrushchev, the man he called "*abuelo*," or "grandfather." The Soviet Union's shipment of small arms, howitzers, and tanks had helped Castro overcome the brigadistas. Against the United States, he expected bigger equipment.

Castro later said, "We planted the idea of an American invasion of Cuba with the Soviets, and the idea of the measures they should take in order to avoid it. . . . That was how the idea of establishing missiles in Cuba came about."

If Castro sought protection for his tiny country, Khrushchev thought in global terms. He later wrote, "We had to think up some way of confronting America with more than words. We had to establish a tangible and effective deterrent to American interference in the Caribbean. But what exactly? The logical answer was missiles."

After meeting President Kennedy in June 1961, Khrushchev concluded that he "could be intimidated and blackmailed." He reasoned that Kennedy would do nothing about missiles already installed and pointed toward the United States.

Soviet ships carrying medium-range and nuclear-warhead missiles and launch site materials headed to Cuba. Although Moscow assured Washington that its shipments did not include offensive weapons, Soviet troops and MiGs arrived on the island. By month's end, an American U-2 reconnaissance flight finally discovered the missile sites under construction.

Kennedy's secretary of state, Dean Rusk, called the six days in October the "most dangerous crisis the world has ever seen." Once the confrontation escalated between the "big dogs," Castro, figuratively speaking, was left on the porch. Curiously, Castro seemed unaware of the dangerous situation. Twenty-five years later, he said, "At that time, I ignored how many nuclear weapons the Soviets had and how many nuclear weapons the North Americans had. . . . We did not have all the information to be able to make a complete evaluation of the situation."

The October 14 reconnaissance photographs revealed a launchpad, buildings, and a missile on the ground in Cuba. With ranges up to 2,000 miles (3,219 kilometers), the nuclear weapons could strike anywhere from Salt Lake City to New York City. Kennedy realized that the missiles could be operational in ten days, not enough time to call a United Nations debate or consult allies. Resolving the crisis fell to the president alone. The administration moved 100,000 troops and aircraft to Florida. An amphibious task force swelled to 40,000 marines, with 5,000 at Guantánamo Bay Naval Base. An additional 14,000 reservists were called up. Yet, Kennedy realized a military strike could kill some 42,000 Soviet advisors and uncounted innocent Cubans.

Then, the U.S. defense secretary, Robert McNamara, proposed a naval blockade as an alternative. Ninety ships, eight carriers, and aircraft squadrons moved to intercept Soviet ships en route to Cuba.

Kennedy's address to the American people on October 22 explained the Soviet threat, the naval quarantine, and his demand that the missiles be removed. He announced that missiles launched from Cuba would be viewed as an attack by the Soviet Union on the United States. He appealed to Khrushchev "to abandon this course of world domination."

That night, Castro prepared for war, mobilizing soldiers, militias, women, and the elderly. "What have we done?" he asked on television. "We have defended ourselves. That is all!"

Four days later, after exchanging messages with Kennedy several times, Khrushchev agreed to remove the missiles. He stopped the Soviet ships from crossing the blockade line. Had they sailed on, American ships would have stopped and boarded them. The Soviet Union would have retaliated against this universal act of war. Each move would have inspired an

This U.S. Department of Defense photograph from November 5, 1962, shows Soviet missile equipment being loaded at the Mariel naval port in Cuba. The Cuban Missile Crisis, a tense standoff between the United States and the Soviet Union in October 1962, led to the removal of Soviet ballistic missiles from Cuba.

even more serious response until the two countries unleashed their most dangerous weapons. A nuclear holocaust might well have occurred.

Back from the brink of destruction, the superpowers relaxed. Two days later, an American U-2 was shot down by a Soviet surface-to-air missile. Castro claimed his men fired only low-altitude antiaircraft weapons: "But a Russian there—and for me it is still a mystery, I don't know whether the Soviet battery chief caught the spirit of our artillerymen and fired, too, or whether he received an order—did fire the rockets."

Fortunately, both superpowers concluded that a local Soviet commander pushed the button without authorization. Had the two sides not overlooked the incident, the United States would likely have fired nuclear warheads into Cuba the next morning.

Castro was furious when the two superpowers came to an agreement. He sent a telegram to Khrushchev, urging a "preemptive" strike against the United States. Castro's risking nuclear war for assurances that the United States would not invade Cuba would have been costly. What would have remained of Cuba for the United States to invade after a nuclear attack? Later, he said, "I never considered the withdraw solution." Excluded from the U.S.-Soviet negotiations, he could not lobby for the removal of the United States' economic blockade or the return of the Guantánamo Bay Naval Base to Cuba. Still, Castro benefited from the crisis. The United States promised not to invade Cuba. The Cuban people again rallied around Castro. His stature in the international community grew.

9

Intervening in the Third World

Cuba's need for Soviet economic and military aid blunted Castro's anger at Khrushchev. He desperately needed the aid. In turn, the Soviet leader needed Castro's good graces inside the circle of Third World nations.

Castro's trip to the Soviet Union in April 1963 served both countries well. For his part, Castro charmed the Soviets with his speeches. For theirs, the Soviets awarded him medals and invited him to speak at Red Square, a high honor for a leader of a small nation of only 8 million people.

In private talks, Castro insisted that Khrushchev's snub during the missile crisis entitled Cuba to more assistance. Eventually, the Soviets agreed to buy Cuba's sugar for five years at a price guaranteed above the world market.

At the same time, Castro steadfastly sidestepped old-line

Fidel Castro, shown cutting sugarcane in a government photograph from February 1961. Castro pushed to increase sugar production in Cuba from 3.8 million tons in 1963 to a goal of 10 million tons by 1970, but the effort fell vastly short.

communism. Castro's version of Marxism-Leninism, he told biographer Tad Szulc, combined elements from Communist and socialist ideas. "I think that salaries are paid according to the work and capacity [a socialist concept]," he said. "But education, for example, universal and generalized, is free. . . . Medical services are received in an egalitarian form by the whole population [a Communist concept]."

At home in Cuba, Castro announced a return to sugar as the sole crop industry. In reality, the government's disorganization and the farmers' inexperience with other crops had proved disastrous. He raised the country's sugar quota from 3.8 million tons in 1963 to 10 million tons by 1970. Cuba's new goals, he said, required people in the cities and the revolutionary army to work in the cane fields. His third agrarian reform in October gave the state 75 percent of the land. "We can do it," he said to the nation. "And it is clear to all of us that we must do it." Cuba's faithful accepted the cause.

Further conflict between Cuba and the Soviet Union rested in Castro's insistence that Third World nations use armed revolution to become independent. In 1964 and 1965, Castro sent Che Guevara first to Africa to train and fight with insurgents and then to South America. Cuba also sent arms and supplies to Venezuelan and Argentinean rebels.

After Guevara was captured and executed in Colombia, Castro honored his longtime comrade by naming 1966 "The Year of Revolutionary Solidarity." In January, Castro hosted the first Tricontinental Conference in Havana, with 512 delegates from 82 countries, as well as 64 observers and 77 invited guests, attending. Among them were Vietcong, Guatemalan rebels, radicals from the United States, and the then-unknown Palestine Liberation Organization (PLO). Through the PLO, Cubans traveled to the Middle East, training antigovernment forces in Libya and Algeria, and participating in tank battles in Syria and South Yemen.

Cuban-U.S. animosities continued behind the scenes. As many as 30 U.S.-inspired attempts were made on Castro's life in 1964 and 1965. Castro courted anti-Vietnam sentiments in the United States, inviting 2,500 radicals to visit Cuba. By filling their heads with tales of the revolution and instructions on how to make Molotov cocktails, he hoped they would disrupt the United States from within.

Castro's tap dance across the world stage exhausted the Soviet Union's patience. Despite generous Soviet trade agreements, Castro suggested that Cuba would soon break away from the Soviet Union, its one customer and benefactor. To emphasize its displeasure, the Soviets decreased delivery of oil to a trickle and prolonged talks on new agreements.

Castro quickly got the message. As the rest of the world, including other Communist countries, condemned the Soviet Union's invasion of Czechoslovakia in 1968, Castro supported his benefactor.

Also in 1968, Castro nationalized nearly 60,000 small businesses. Desperate for money, the government seized enterprises such as auto repair shops and ice cream stands. Castro told the people no one had fought a revolution "to establish the right for somebody to make two hundred pesos selling rum or fifty pesos selling fried eggs. . . . Clearly and definitely we must say that we propose to eliminate all manifestations of private trade."

The sugar harvest of 1970 fell 2 million tons short of Castro's promised 10 million tons. For once, Castro did not blame the United States, or the laziness of the people, or exiled Cubans. "I believe that we cost the people too much in our process of learning," he said. Humbled, Castro offered to resign. The masses would not entertain the notion. He turned to the Soviets, even relinquishing some of his authority for help in planning Cuba's economy. A new Cuban-Soviet Commission of Economic, Scientific, and Technical Collaboration studied the Cuban economy and made recommendations.

With Cuba cooperating more fully, the Soviet Union gave its irritating protégé some financial and military breathing room. It offered new trade agreements allowing Cuba to defer payment and interest charges on its $4 billion to $5 billion debt. It also supplied additional MiGs and other military equipment.

In 1974, a more mature Castro considered a more normal Cuban-U.S. relationship. The two countries had entered into a small antihijacking pact the year before, but the larger issues of full diplomatic relations had not changed in 15 years. Castro wanted the trade embargo lifted and the Guantánamo Bay base returned. The United States required compensation for American properties seized in the revolution. The secret talks between Cuba and President Gerald Ford's administration continued for a year, offering some hope for a solution. When Castro sent troops to Angola to support his old friend Agostino Neto, however, the talks ended.

Failure to create an improved relationship with the United States was a small price to pay for the benefits Castro reaped. In the Third World, his reputation had been tarnished by Cuba's dependence on Soviet money and personnel. The Angolan leader's request for troops gave Castro a golden opportunity to redeem himself. He personally handpicked battalion commanders and christened ships carrying 18,000 Cuban troops. The Cubans proved essential in defeating a South African invasion of Neto's new Marxist government. They stayed on to help restructure the government.

Castro's actions in Angola, and later in Ethiopia, helped him at home and abroad. They placed Cuba on the same battlefields as the superpowers. They also provided Cubans with another goal. "There have been generations that have moved through the revolution," a Cuban official said. "The first generation made the revolution in 1959. In 1962, the literacy campaign was for the next wave of kids. Then there was the Great Ten-Million-Ton. This is the revolutionary experience of this generation—the way they receive revolutionary fervor." Castro also earned approval from the United Nations General Assembly for his help in Africa's "national liberation."

In the Western Hemisphere, some members of the OAS individually established diplomatic relations with Cuba. The OAS then voted to readmit Cuba into its group. The Nonaligned Movement, which nearly expelled Cuba from the organization in 1976, invited Castro to host the 1979 summit and chair the organization for three years.

Cuba intervened in Central America as well. It fully supported Nicaragua's revolution. The Sandinista guerrillas, hoping to overthrow the United States–backed dictator, even wore Cuba's revolutionary black and red colors. After

Castro with Sandinista soldiers visiting Cuba in July 1979. With Castro's support, the Sandinista soldiers overthrew the U.S.-backed dictator in Nicaragua. Afterward, Castro sent $200 million in aid.

their 1979 victory, Castro sent advisors, professionals, and $200 million in aid.

Castro's foreign triumphs did not change many Cubans' dissatisfaction with their own lives. The educated and elite continued to leave the country. In April 1980, six Cubans crashed through the gates of the Peruvian Embassy, seeking sanctuary. An angry Castro announced that anyone who could get transportation out of Port Mariel could leave Cuba; some 10,800 Cubans rushed to the embassy. A month later, more than 120,000 Cubans left for the United States in what was known as the Mariel boatlift.

The new exiles revealed an unpleasant inner Cuba. Government officials chose who could leave, permitting only one family member per boat. They released many hardened criminals among the law-abiding citizens. The prisoners told terrible stories of beatings, torture, and plastic surgery with razor blades.

Issues, like fishing rights, boundaries, and exchange of weather information, were resolved between Cuba and the Jimmy Carter administration. Yet neither nation understood the other anymore than it ever did. To restore diplomatic relations, Carter insisted on compensation for American properties—again. Castro insisted on the lifting of the trade embargo—again. The United States hoped to influence Castro's stance on human rights issues and meddling in Africa. Castro saw these conditions as violating Cuban sovereignty—again.

The limited communication that the Carter administration had nurtured with Cuba withered with the "boat people" incident. It ended entirely when Ronald Reagan was elected president in 1980. The Reagan administration halted travel to Cuba and condemned Cuba's African entanglements. It convincingly squelched Castro's plans to turn the tiny island nation of Grenada toward socialism. Acting on the request of the Organization of Eastern Caribbean States, Reagan ordered troops to the Caribbean island in October 1983. Their victory was devastating to the aging revolutionary. "For Castro to accept defeat was impossible," a Cuban-American psychiatrist said. "The image of the invincible cracked right there. It was not a matter that this was a tiny island, it was a matter of being defeated."

In 1985, other factors closed in around Castro. The Reagan administration reached into Castro's domain electronically by erecting Radio Martí. The station broadcast news from the outside world without the bias of Castro's propaganda. Unable to raise enough sugar for the Soviet quota, Castro was forced to buy sugar on the world market and resell it to the Soviets. He proposed a solution to Cuba's money troubles by hosting five conferences on debt crises. Gathering other money-strapped Latin American countries together, he suggested that their

$420 billion debt to the United States and other Western money lenders simply be ignored and never repaid.

The Soviet Union's new leader, Mikhail Gorbachev, pressed Castro to remove Cuba's 57,000 troops from Angola. Their knowledge of weapons and battle, paired with their dissatisfaction of their homeland, threatened Castro's regime. Castro ruthlessly charged a popular war veteran with drug smuggling to discourage any thoughts of a military coup. He arranged the 1989 trial before an illegal military tribunal and illegally convicted General Arnaldo Ochoa with his own testimony. Ochoa met the fate Castro desired: the firing squad. Five months later, American troops overthrew the Castro-supported regime in Panama and arrested Castro's protégé, Manuel Noriega. Eight weeks after Panama's change in government, Nicaraguans voted out another Castro man, Daniel Ortega.

The worst catastrophe for Cuba in 1989 was the beginning of the collapse of the Soviet Union. With the loss of its biggest customer and benefactor, Cuba's hard economic times have continued to the present. The production of sugarcane, which covers 72 percent of Cuba's cultivatable land, sank to 3.5 million tons in 2000 and sold for world market prices of about five cents a pound. Another current dominant source of income for Cuba is tourism, sustained by 2 million Canadian, Mexican, and Spanish visitors each year. The recent wave of terrorism and world conflicts has reduced vacationing, however.

U.S. President George W. Bush still maintains the traditional hard line on Cuba. Supporting the embargo's status quo, some people charge that Castro is still an enemy of the United States. They believe Cuba is a spy center for passing intelligence about the United States to potential enemies. They emphasize Castro's effort toward building an alliance of rogue states, including Libya, Syria, and Iran. They point out that in May 2001, he said, "Iran and Cuba, in cooperation with each other, can bring America to its knees." They worry

A tour bus passes farmers harvesting sugarcane in Guardalavaca in May 2001. Sugar production fell to 3.5 million tons by 2000. Cuban officials hope tourism will save the country's faltering economy.

that Cuba's biological research facility is capable of producing chemical and biological weapons.

Others in the United States criticize past confrontational policy. They argue that it has not forced Castro out of Cuba for four decades. They also point out that Castro himself has done less fist-pounding in recent years. After the September 11, 2001, attacks on New York and Washington, D.C., Castro endorsed antiterrorism treaties. He said nothing when Al Qaeda and Taliban prisoners were taken to the Guantánamo Bay Naval Base. Once the world's biggest renegade, Castro even offered to return escapees to the facility. Castro has also proposed a joint effort between Cuba and the United States to ferret out drug traffic. Castro invited former President Jimmy Carter to visit Cuba in May 2002.

The passage of a 2000 reform bill in Congress that allows

Cuba to purchase food and medicine on a cash-only basis has opened the door for trade between the United States and Cuba. Castro also hosted a trade show in Havana, where he purchased $120 million in products, pleasing U.S. farmers.

Still, the government's attitude has remained firm. In 2002, during a celebration of the hundredth anniversary of Cuba's independence, President George W. Bush called Castro a "tyrant who uses brutal methods to enforce a bankrupt vision." Bush urged Castro to obey the Cuban constitution and hold free elections. If Castro instituted meaningful reforms, Bush pledged to "work with the United States Congress to ease the ban on trade and travel."

10

Writing in the History Books

"History has not given the final word," Fidel Castro told a Spanish official who asked if Castro's moment in history had passed. Castro has ruled his country longer than any other current world leader, except for Great Britain's Queen Elizabeth II. He has dealt with ten U.S. presidents and five Soviet premiers. He has seen countries created and countries destroyed, some with his influence.

Whether life in Cuba is better now than under the previous governments is uncertain. Before Castro took power in 1959, Cuba's resources were concentrated on making Havana a lush vacation center for the rich. Rural Cubans lived in terrible conditions. Seventy-five percent lived in huts made of palm trees, without sanitation, running water, and electricity. Health care was nonexistent. The ratio of physicians to people was only one to 2,000. School was not

Fidel Castro during a ceremony to inaugurate a new school year in September 2002. Many observers wonder what will happen when the aging leader can no longer stay in power.

attended by 27 percent of urban children and 61 percent of rural children. Nearly half of the adult peasants were illiterate. There were no rural roads. Officials pocketed money from the national treasury. There were no free elections. Dissidents were thrown in jail without a trial. Torture and murder were common in the prisons.

As the ultimate revolutionary, Castro possessed the will, the energy, and the cunning to overthrow the government that created these conditions. His socialist government built roads.

Today, however, only one in 50 Cubans has a car to use those roads or the money to pay for gas at about $4 a gallon. In 2003, Castro told an NBC reporter that Cuba did not import cars because their tires and spare parts caused too much trouble. His government provided new housing. But today, shortages sometimes require two families to share the same apartment.

Castro's national literacy campaign opened more schools during the first 30 months of his rule than in the previous 30 years. Today, every child must participate in the government's free education. More than 95 percent of adult Cubans are literate. Yet newspapers are controlled by the state. The government also controls radio and television. Only one person in five owns a radio, and one in 13 owns a television.

Castro's socialist government ousted foreign companies and seized control of all industry. In 1987, nearly three decades after Castro came to power, the average Cuban's income was about $90 a month. Beef, detergent, sugar, underwear, shampoo, and other basic necessities were rationed. Fifteen years later, in the twenty-first century, Cubans earned only about $10 a month. They shopped at government stores for government-approved kitchen utensils, lamps, and wedding dresses. Food was still rationed. Critics charge that the government is nearly bankrupt, while Castro hides $1.5 billion in secret Swiss accounts.

Like the Batista government that Castro overthrew, Castro's government allows no freedom of speech, religion, press, or right to assembly. In a 2003 interview, he argued that these freedoms should not be forced on people who do not want them. Activists are held without trial for indefinite periods, are sentenced to labor camps, or simply disappear. The Communist Party of Cuba is the only political party, and 400,000 Cubans are members.

Castro, the ultimate soldier, has waged a continual verbal and political war with his archenemy, the United States. The 40-year-old trade embargo has served him well. It keeps the United States out, and keeps the people of Cuba isolated within. "The Cuban government doesn't actually want the embargo to be lifted," Cuba's leading human rights campaigner says. "The sanctions policy has given the government a good alibi to justify the failure of the totalitarian model."

Still, Castro's hold on Cuba's masses is ironclad. Men, women, and children cried when he fainted during a June 2001 speech. "A future without Castro is too frightening to even speak. . . . They don't like to say 'death' and 'Castro' in the same sentence," a *Dallas Morning News* correspondent wrote. "They say, 'when Fidel ceases to exist physically.'" A year later, a million Cubans marched with Castro, protesting the constitutional provision that might force him to hold free elections and improve their lives.

Nearly 80 years old, Castro has named his brother as his successor. Yet many doubt Raúl's ability to continue Fidel's socialist regime. Some believe a completely new government will arise after Castro's death. Others hope for a popular uprising to overthrow him even before he dies.

Many of those who lived through Castro's great revolution are gone. Younger generations know only the hardships of his tight-fisted control. Yet Fidel Castro's ultimate contribution to Cuba may be giving Cuba back its dignity. As a leader of a small island who influenced actions of more powerful nations, Castro helped Cubans regain pride in themselves and in their country. He wrested his country from those who controlled Cuba militarily and economically. Whatever Cuba is like today is the result of decisions made by a Cuban about Cuba, not by a distant overseer nation.

There is only one Fidel Castro. He would not be ruled by another country. He would not be squeezed into any political label. Still wearing the combat fatigues and the beard of the revolutionary, he is already described in history books as one of the most intriguing leaders of our time. How much more will be added to his story remains to be seen.

1926	Fidel Castro Ruz is born on August 13 near Biran, Cuba.
1945	Enters School of Law at the University of Havana.
1947	Joins attempted invasion of the Dominican Republic to overthrow the dictator Rafael Trujillo.
1948	In April, participates in riots in Bogotá, Colombia; on October 12, marries Mirta Diaz-Balart.
1949	Son, Fidel "Fidelito" Castro Diaz-Balart, is born September 14.
1950	Graduates from the University of Havana with a law degree.
1952	In March, General Fulgencio Batista overthrows the government and cancels elections.
1953	On July 26, leads an attack on the Moncada military barracks.
1953–1955	Serves prison sentence on Isle of Pines.
1955–1956	Trains a revolutionary group of Cuban exiles in Mexico.
1956	In December, lands in the Oriente Province with 81 men.
1956–1959	Fights Fulgencio Batista's troops for control of government.
1959	On January 1, Batista's government falls; in February, becomes commander-in-chief and premier with Manuel Urrutia as president.
1959	In July, assumes complete control of the government.
1960	In February, makes trade agreement with the Soviet Union, severing economic ties with the United States.
1961	In January, breaks diplomatic relations with the United States; in April, crushes U.S.-backed Bay of Pigs invasion.
1962	In October, Cuban Missile Crisis threatens nuclear war.
1975	Sends troops into Angolan civil war.
1976	Creates a new constitution and a National Assembly; becomes president of the State Council.
1980	Emerges as a leader of Third World countries; allows those who want to leave Cuba to do so.

1987 Agrees to keep "undesirable" immigrants in Cuba.

1991 Loses subsidies from the Soviet Union with its collapse.

1998 Visited by Pope John Paul II.

2001 Purchases food from the United States for the first time in 40 years.

2002 Visited by former U.S. President Jimmy Carter.

Balfour, Sebastian, *Castro (Profiles in Power)*. New York: Longman, 2000.

Bunck, Julie Marie, *Fidel Castro and the Quest for a Revolutionary Culture in Cuba*. University Park: Pennsylvania State University Press, 1994.

Castro, Fidel, with Deborah Shnookel and Pedro Alvarez Tabio, eds., *My Early Years*. New York: Ocean Press, 1998.

Fernandez, Damian J., *Cuba and the Politics of Passion*. Austin: University of Texas Press, 2000.

Foss, Clive, *Fidel Castro (Sutton Pocket Biographies)*. Phoenix Mill, England: Sutton Publishing, 2000.

Geyer, Georgie Anne, *Guerrilla Prince: The Untold Story of Fidel Castro*. Boston: Little, Brown and Company, 1991.

Montaner, Carlos Alberto, *Journey to the Heart of Cuba—Life as Fidel Castro*. New York: Algora Publishers, 2001.

Moses, Catherine, *Real Life in Castro's Cuba*. Wilmington, DE: Scholarly Resources, 1999.

Oppenheimer, Andres, *Castro's Final Hour: The Secret Story Behind the Coming Downfall of Communist Cuba*. New York: Touchstone Books, 1993.

Perez-Stable, Marifeli, *The Cuban Revolution: Origins, Course, and Legacy*. New York: Oxford University Press, 1997.

Quirk, Robert E., *Fidel Castro*. New York: W.W. Norton & Company, 1995.

Suchlicki, Jaime, *Cuba: From Columbus to Castro and Beyond*. London: Brasseys Publishing, 1997.

Szulc, Tad, *Fidel: A Critical Portrait*. New York: Avon Books, 2000.

INDEX

page:

2:   AFP/NMI
11: 21st Century Publishing
13: AP/Wide World Photos
16: Charles Tasnadi/AP/
     Wide World Photos
21: New Millennium Images
24: © CORBIS
27: © Bettmann/CORBIS
31: AP/Wide World Photos
34: EFE/AP/Wide World Photos
37: Diario De La Marina/AP/
     Wide World Photos
40: AP/Wide World Photos
43: Bettmann/CORBIS
45: AP/Wide World Photos
50: AP/Wide World Photos
53: © Tim Page/CORBIS
57: © Bettmann/CORBIS

61: Andrew St. George/AP/
     Wide World Photos
66: © Bettmann/CORBIS
70: Andrew St. George/AP/
     Wide World Photos
73: AP/Wide World Photos
76: AP/Wide World Photos
80: AP/Wide World Photos
82: AP/Wide World Photos
87: Doug Kennedy/AP/Wide World Photos
89: AP/Wide World Photos
93: Canadian Press Photo/AP/
     Wide World Photos
98: AP/Wide World Photos
101: AP/Wide World Photos
105: AP/Wide World Photos
108: Cristobal Herrera/AP/Wide World Photos
111: AFP/NMI

Cover: Canadian Press Photo/AP/Wide World Photos

VICKI COX writes freelance for newspapers and magazines in 16 states. *Rising Stars and Ozark Constellations* is her anthology of people and places in the Midwest. Ms. Cox has an M.S. in education and has taught for 25 years. She teaches at Drury University in Springfield, Missouri, and frequently speaks at writer and education conferences. She lives in Lebanon, Missouri.

ARTHUR M. SCHLESINGER, JR. is the leading American historian of our time. He won the Pulitzer Prize for his book *The Age of Jackson* (1945) and again for a chronicle of the Kennedy administration, *A Thousand Days* (1965), which also won the National Book Award. Professor Schlesinger is the Albert Schweitzer Professor of the Humanities at the City University of New York and has been involved in several other Chelsea House projects, including the series REVOLUTIONARY WAR LEADERS, COLONIAL LEADERS, and YOUR GOVERNMENT.